Dafydd
ap Llywelyn
The Shield of Wales

Dafydd
ap Llywelyn
The Shield of Wales

Steve Griffiths

I dedicate this book to the joint memory of my late grandfathers:
Thomas Charles Hough of Connah's Quay, Deeside, Flintshire
and John Richard Griffiths of Llaneilian, Amlwch, Sir Fôn.

First impression: 2011
Second impression: 2011
© Steve Griffiths & Y Lolfa Cyf., 2011

Photographs: Steve Griffiths
Cover design: Y Lolfa

ISBN: 9781847713384

FSC
Published and printed in Wales
on paper from well managed forests by
Y Lolfa Cyf., Talybont, Ceredigion SY24 5HE
e-mail ylolfa@ylolfa.com
website www.ylolfa.com
tel 01970 832 304
fax 832 782

A nation with no knowledge of it's history is akin to a man who has lost his own memory.

Gwynfor Evans

Introduction

Prince Dafydd ap Llywelyn was the second born son of the greatly revered Welsh prince, Llywelyn ap Iorwerth – better known to the majority of historians as Prince Llywelyn the Great, Prince of Aberffraw and Lord of Snowdon. Dafydd was born at the Welsh royal residence of Castell Hen Blas in the borderlands of northern Flintshire; and by being born to an English mother of royal blood, he initially attracted the mistrust and enmity of a large proportion of his fellow countrymen. However, after the death of his widely respected father, Dafydd confidently embarked upon his own individual quest for glory and fulfilment – blazing a colourful trail in his wake of fraternal strife, political intrigue, periodic warfare, temporary triumph, daring adventure and finally the sufferance of a mysterious and premature death during the tender years of his early thirties. Much more importantly, Dafydd is renowned as being the first Welsh royal leader who confidently invested himself to the supreme title of Prince of Wales. Dafydd ap Llywelyn ap Iorwerth, or Prince Dafydd the Second of Gwynedd and Wales, deserves to be placed alongside those other great Welsh rulers of the Mediaeval age, including Hywel Dda, Rhodri Mawr, the two Llywelyns and Owain Glyndŵr and this account shall hopefully encourage such a defining prospect, aiding the campaign for his seemingly obscure name to be finally included within the realm of the modern-day Welsh psyche.

– I –

Prince Dafydd ap Llywelyn was born at his father's royal residence in the manor of Coleshill in Flintshire sometime during or around the year 1215, where an established royal court belonging to the Welsh princes once stood called Castell Hen Blas. Once a vibrant mediaeval manor, the modern day area that is Coleshill currently forms a part of the Flintshire village of Bagillt, a small, close-knit community that is somewhat overshadowed by the heavily populated neighbouring town of Flint. The district's present day terrain yields the distinctive scar tissue of modern man's industrious endeavour to grapple with coal, lead, steel and textile, but the luscious sloping meadows that still dominate the fertile landscape alongside the Dee estuary would undoubtedly have formed a picturesque setting and an idyllic backdrop for such an occasion as an important and prestigious royal birth.

Dafydd ap Llywelyn was the second and final born son of the revered Welsh prince, Llywelyn ap Iorwerth – The Great (reigned 1200–40), and in historical terms Dafydd is widely recognised as being the only male member of the royal dynasty of Gwynedd to have been born inside the boundaries of Tegeingl – a Welsh *cantref* or district of the mediaeval period now roughly defined as the modern-day county of Flintshire. The *cantref* of Tegeingl or Englefield in English in north-east Wales could already boast of important contributions to Welsh royal society, in particular two female members belonging to the district's minor royal house – with its chief ancestral seat rooted at the Llys Edwin fortification in Northop (Llaneurgain) – had previously become royal consorts to former rulers of Gwynedd. Angharad married King Gruffydd ap Cynan (*c.*1054–1137) and Cristin married Prince Owain Gwynedd (*c.*1100–70). Dafydd's English mother, Joan, was an illegitimate daughter of King John of England (reigned 1199–1216) and during the year 1205, the fresh-faced teenage princess, Lady Joan of England became Princess Siwan (Joan) of Gwynedd and Wales when she exchanged wedding vows with Prince Llywelyn ap Iorwerth inside the holy precincts of the principal church of Chester. Therefore, through the bloodline of his English mother, the newborn Dafydd had inherited the distinguished plasma of English royalty. Dafydd had a half-brother, Gruffydd, who was some ten years or more his senior and had been spawned from Prince Llywelyn's previous relationship with the red-headed beauty, Tangwystl Goch.

Directly descended from William the Conqueror, the Norman-French king who ruled England between the years 1066–87, Dafydd was also the maternal grandson of King John; a great nephew of Richard the Lionheart (ruled as King of England 1189–99) and later he would become the older first cousin to Edward the First (ruled as King of England 1272–1307). By being born to an English mother of royal blood, Dafydd expectedly attracted the enmity and mistrust of a proportion of his fellow countrymen, many of whom preferred instead to pledge their allegiance towards the opposing corner of Gruffydd, Dafydd's illegitimate and elder born half-brother of pure Welsh stock.

For the first twenty years or so of his youngest son's life, Prince Llywelyn conducted a determined campaign to secure Dafydd's status as his chosen heir and designated successor, to the detriment of his disjointed firstborn son, Gruffydd. The unprecedented campaign proved successful and the lack of any serious open opposition from the Welsh ruling order allowed the initiative to impregnate the political landscape of Gwynedd on three distinct occasions. During the year 1220, King Henry the Third of England (reigned 1216–72), together with his archbishop, Stephen Langton, initially acknowledged the young Dafydd as Prince Llywelyn's chosen heir; and again, during the year 1222, the ruling pope, Honorius the Third, reaffirmed Dafydd's position as heir-apparent; and finally, during October of 1238, a great national assembly was convened at the Cistercian abbey of Strata Florida in Dyfed where the lesser Welsh princes collectively swore fealty towards Dafydd. Beyond all reasonable doubt, Dafydd was now primed as a leader-in-waiting.

On the 19th of October 1216, Dafydd's grandfather, King John of England, died at the Nottinghamshire castle of Newark. The kingdom of England then passed on to his son, Henry who, some nine days later, was crowned King Henry the Third of England. Born at Winchester on the 1st of October 1207, the eldest son of King John and his second wife, Isabella, ascended the throne when he was just nine years of age. The boy king would later grow to become an intensely cultured man, and his passion for the arts led to the rebuilding of the magnificent Gothic abbey of Westminster. England had gladly inherited a king, but much more ominously for Dafydd – himself still entwined within the bosom of infanthood, the kingdom of Gwynedd had unwittingly inherited a future enemy. In the meantime, the biggest threat posed to the stability of the Welsh Kingdom of Gwynedd proved to be much closer to home. During the year 1228, Llywelyn's eldest son, the illegitimate Gruffydd – a man renowned for his troublesome temperament and ungovernable spirit – was upon the precipice of elevating his own princely status by the most dramatic of means. From his royal court of Nefyn upon the Llŷn peninsula, Gruffydd was planning to execute a stunning coup de theatre against the balance of power in Gwynedd. However, the seemingly violent plot was successfully thwarted before its fruition. Hearing news of the revolt, Prince Llywelyn acted decisively and ordered the immediate arrest and subsequent detention of his rebellious son. Satisfied by the urgency of his actions, Llywelyn then forcibly banished the fiery Gruffydd to the custodial confinement of Deganwy Castle. For the next two years, and with Gruffydd securely held beneath lock and key inside the prominent quarters upon the rugged hilltop beside the Conwy estuary, family life for the royal family of Gwynedd was seemingly blessed with absolute harmony. That is, until the manifestation of a shocking domestic incident, which in turn would create a royal scandal of the greatest magnitude.

Ever since the historic event of the Battle of Hastings of 1066, and the subsequent successful Norman conquest of Saxon England, the border region that lay sandwiched between Wales and England had become saturated with a large influx of powerful Norman barons who, together with their war-mongering families, voraciously craved for further and future conquests. This geographical region of Norman residency became known as the Marcher Lands. The native Welsh princes came under considerable and extensive threat from this latest, troublesome ogre from the east and, in a determined quest to preserve the guarded trappings of their own elevated status and wealth, a number of the dynastic rulers duly courted the alliance of this fearsome and all-powerful "new-age" Norman nobility. The widely respected Welsh ruler, Lord Rhys ap Gruffydd of the kingdom of Deheubarth (reigned 1155–97), who had stood at the head of the powerful royal house of Dinefwr in southern Wales, successfully adopted this very policy during his lifetime by him arranging convenient marriages of alliance between his own offspring and selected members drawn form the Anglo-Norman aristocracy, thereby preserving the hegemony of the family bloodline. The royal house of Gwynedd in northern Wales did not differ to those other royal houses of mediaeval Welsh Wales in this respect, its members also negotiating inter-racial marriages as a means to them cementing crucial alliances. Evidence suggests that from the closing years of the twelfth century until the eventual disintegration of the northern house of Aberffraw (Gwynedd) at the end of the thirteenth century, at least six members belonging to its senior ranks – five of whom achieved the status of ruling prince – chose women of Anglo-Norman extraction to be their endowed consort. As follows: Dafydd the First (d. 1203) married Emma of Anjou – a half-sister of King Henry the Second; Llywelyn the Great (d. 1240) married Joan – an illegitimate daughter of King John of England; Dafydd the Second (d. 1246) married Isabella – a daughter of Lord William de Braose; Llywelyn ap Gruffydd (d. 1282) married Eleanor – a daughter of Simon de Montfort, Earl of Leicester; Dafydd the Third (d. 1283) married Elizabeth de Ferrers – a daughter of the Earl of Derby, and Rhodri ap Gruffydd (d. 1315) married Beatrice – a daughter of the Earl of Malpas.

Despite the consistency of these important alliances of marriage, problems would continue to erupt between the Norman settlers and their descendants and those influential native residents whom they still wished to overwhelm and conquer. Of all the Anglo-Norman families who had settled upon Welsh soil, none came to symbolise the fragile and often fractured relationship between the two races than the example of the ruthless clan of de Braose. The infamous William de Braose (d. 1211), an Anglo-Norman baron whose lands, which included the lordships of Builth and Brycheiniog, he and his family had acquired via the medium of force and fear, was held responsible for the detonation of the opening salvo of hostilities when he maliciously lured unsuspecting members of the Welsh nobility of Upland Gwent to his Abergavenny Castle base under the guise of an intended peace conference during the year 1175. Already renowned for his brutish nature, the notoriously vile Marcher lord successfully duped Seisyll ap Dyfnwal and other local elders into attending a conference listed as peace talks. Once securely inside the closed gates of the castle, the Welsh delegation of nobles were savagely butchered by de Braose's heavily-armed reception committee, earning the deeply despised de Braose the lifetime nickname of the "Ogre of Abergavenny".

Almost six decades had elapsed since the mournful occasion of the notorious massacre of Abergavenny before the infamous name of de Braose would once again manufacture an indelible imprint upon the blood-soaked pages of Welsh history. During this period, the strained relationship between the respective kingdom entities of Gwynedd and England could be regarded as anything other than cordial. The rare harmony created by an uninterrupted three year period of peace was abruptly shattered during the opening weeks of September 1228, when an episode of fresh hostilities erupted in the location of the densely wooded borderland forests of Powys. The frontier zone became a killing ground as it hosted a fresh series of skirmishes between Welsh and English forces to which a certain William de Braose (d. 1230) – a descendant of the despised, but by now deceased William de Braose the Elder (d. 1211) – figured as a prominent commander of the campaigning English soldiery. However, during the occasion of what was described by contemporary accounts as a series of "fierce attacks", a band of Welsh troops, led by Prince Llywelyn ap Iorwerth, delivered a crushing defeat to an English military detachment at the Welsh border lordship of Ceri (Kerry), near Newtown. The inglorious trouncing suffered by the English force was further amplified by the news of the capture of the notable William de Braose, a son of Reginald de Braose. His force resoundingly defeated, the badly wounded, eminent prisoner-of-war was hurriedly dispatched northwards to Gwynedd, where be would enter the secure confinement of its royal court. After spending almost one full year in captivity as the personal prisoner of Prince Llywelyn, de Braose was then ransomed and released for a sum of £2,000, this figure being a truly astronomical sum for the period.

William de Braose's enforced period of confinement within the remote quarters of Gwynedd had gladly presented Prince Llywelyn with an ample opportunity to formulate an alliance between the principal royal house of Wales and a powerful lord of the March. Neither party hesitated and, as part of the agreed terms of the new pact, de Braose obediently pledged the hand of his daughter, Isabella, in marriage towards Llywelyn's youngest son, Dafydd. Once his wounds of battle had adequately healed, de Braose was then released as Llywelyn's obliging ally.

However, a trusted ally de Braose was certainly not, and he caused a royal scandal of the greatest degree by the very nature of his indefensible conduct whilst lodged in the care of the royal court of Prince Llywelyn. During the occasion of his personal visit to the royal court of Garth Celyn, Abergwyngregyn, near Bangor, in order to formulate final arrangements for the impending marriage, de Braose would undoubtedly have received the full warmth of Welsh royal hospitality and been the grateful recipient of all he wanted by way of food, beverage and accommodation. Nevertheless, the Anglo-Norman lord disgracefully breached royal protocol when he was shockingly discovered inside the private bedchambers of Princess Joan's royal apartments. Princess Joan, or Siwan in Welsh, was fast approaching her years of middle age, and after twenty-five years of dutiful marriage to Llywelyn, she had dramatically succumbed to the alluring temptation of a younger man, a figure who must have possessed the highly impressionable qualities of being dashing, articulate and well dressed, and for his part, had successfully charmed himself into the royal bed of the First Lady of Wales.

Upon the detection of their most intimate deed during the Easter of 1230, the shamefaced couple were separated and then instantly detained to await the fate of Prince Llywelyn's personal judgement. Retribution from the justly enraged Welsh prince was delivered one month later when de Braose was sentenced to death upon the decree of Llywelyn's royal council. The execution was conducted in full view of up to eight hundred of Llywelyn's local subjects who witnessed first hand the dishonourable de Braose bear the public indignity of being hung directly above the sewage pit at Llys Garth Celyn. According to local tradition, the knowledge of the exact location of William de Braose's inglorious descent towards stench and death has somehow survived the centuries; visitors to the modern-day site that currently occupies the ancient royal court of Garth Celyn are duly informed of the precise spot still known today as "Hanging Marsh". Upon Llywelyn's personal command, the lifeless body of the adulterous Marcher lord was hacked down and briskly removed from the royal court to be interred within a secluded cave upon a nearby mountain, some four miles south of Garth Celyn. Again, this area can still be positively identified by the local tradition of an aptly named field called "Cae Gwilym Ddu", meaning "Black William's Field".

The public execution on the 2nd of May 1230, of a prominent Marcher lord, condemned to death by the jurisdiction of a Welsh jury who had assertively delivered the damning indictment upon the sanctuary of Welsh soil should, under normal circumstances, have sent shockwaves reverberating throughout the English royal court. Instead, the anticipated response from the corridors of power in London was strangely muted. The Crown's solitary response to the issue of the whole sorry saga emanated via a letter almost three months later, in which the English royal court declared that the unfortunate episode was to be defined as a domestic incident and should be considered as a topic of nobody else's primary concern. Prince Llywelyn would later write to William de Braose's grieving widow, Eva, duly informing her that it had been virtually impossible for him to personally intervene in order to halt the Welsh wheels of justice mid-motion; and any personal attempt he could possibly have undertaken in order to restrain the will and duty of his senior royal council would have proved futile considering the extent of anger and outrage that the scandal had created. Within the same fabric of Llywelyn's personal correspondence to Lady Eva de Braose, the Welsh prince asked specifically for the distressed widow's personal permission for the intended marriage of their kin to continue as planned. With her daughter, Isabella, still in temporary residence at the Welsh royal court, Eva was faced with little alternative but to reluctantly submit to Llywelyn's wish. Thereafter, plans for the royal ceremony proceeded beneath the controversial smear of the darkest of clouds.

During the year 1234, and some four years after the dramatic episode of domestic turmoil had surpassed, Llywelyn's eldest son, Gruffydd, was released from the restraints of his custodial quarters at Deganwy Castle. Gladly returning from the isolated wilderness, the paroled Gruffydd was immediately granted one half of the lordship of Llŷn in north-west Wales, and over the course of the next three years the reconciliation between the father and his strong-spirited son was further reinforced by Llywelyn granting his eldest born the remaining portion of Llŷn, together with the whole of southern Powys. However, from Dafydd's personal viewpoint, the dark shadow of suspicion and mistrust that the aura of his elder brother had always attracted would never truly disappear despite the fact of Gruffydd's latest return to favour and fortune.

During February 1237, the rapidly ageing Llywelyn – now approaching his sixty-fifth year of life and growing ever wearisome from the enterprising effects of almost four entire decades of strenuous and successful rule – suffered the personal trauma of the death of his beloved wife, Princess Joan (Siwan). Beyond all reasonable doubt, the First Lady of Gwynedd and Wales had in fact been pardoned for the misdemeanors incurred during her immoral role in the shocking de Braose scandal and, enjoying the benefit of being officially pardoned, the princess herself had specifically chosen the golden shores of Mona (Anglesey) as her preferred burial place, instead of her choosing an obscure and easily forgotten crypt in distant England. The body of Llywelyn's English-born wife of thirty-two years was lavishly entombed within the priory of Llanfaes, near Beaumaris, a Franciscan settlement that had been purposely constructed for the safe detainment of her mortal remains. The sacred burial plot at Llanfaes commanded a perfect vantage point for the benefit of Llys Garth Celyn upon the opposite shoreline. Standing at a direct distance of only four miles across the Straits of Menai, Princess Joan's magnificent seashore mausoleum would have been the very first sight that greeted the grieving eyes of Prince Llywelyn upon his rising each morning at Llys Garth Celyn. The traumatic event of his wife's death accelerated the prince towards the dawn of his very own demise, as, during that same year (1237) Llywelyn went on to suffer the occurrence of a paralytic stroke. Worse followed this event, when the unpredictable Gruffydd chose that precise moment to decidedly rebel once again against the dual interests of the terminally ill Llywelyn and his strong-willed heir-apparent, Dafydd.

Map illustration of regional and local divisions in mediaeval Wales

In Conwy there stands a statue to Prince Llywelyn the Great. The highly respected prince of Gwynedd ruled his realm between the years 1200–40.

Castell Hen Blas Castle, Coleshill, Bagillt, Flintshire

Hen Blas was a site of huge importance during the mediaeval age and it is believed that it was first occupied as early as the 9th century. During the year 1157, King Henry the Second of England claimed the site and transformed the ancient pile into an English royal castle to become one of three such royal castles in the area, the others being at Rhuddlan and Prestatyn. It later fell to Welsh forces during the year 1166 and thereon was used as a royal household that served the royal families of Gwynedd until their eventual extinction. The royal *llys* at Castell Hen Blas was the birthplace of Prince Dafydd ap Llywelyn during or around the year 1215, and to commemorate this important royal birth, his father, Prince Llywelyn ap Iorwerth, erected a chapel close to the vicinity of the royal court.

Llys Edwin, Llaneurgain (Northop), Flintshire

The former residence and chief manorial court of the mediaeval lords of Tegeingl, the blood relatives and long-standing allies of the royal House of Gwynedd.

19

Top Left: "The Royal Lions of Gwynedd" – The coat-of-arms, symbolic of the royal house of Gwynedd, was first used by Llywelyn the Great and later embraced by his son and successor, Dafydd ap Llywelyn.

Top Right: Dafydd's secondary coat-of-arms. "Three roundels Vert; a chief dancetty Vert a lion passant Sable" are attributed to Dafydd in an ancient manuscript written by the 13th century chronicler, Matthew Paris. The distinctive coat-of-arms appears nowhere else, either in contemporary or later sources.

Bottom Left: "The Eagles of Snowdon" – The coat-of-arms of Prince Owain Gwynedd (d. 1170), ruler of Gwynedd 1137–70. Owain was the great-grandfather of Prince Dafydd ap Llywelyn.

Bottom Right: Three lions passant. The coat-of-arms of King Gruffydd ap Cynan, ruler of North Wales 1081–1137. Gruffydd was the great, great-grandfather of Prince Dafydd ap Llywelyn.

The Welsh princes were often called lions and sometimes eagles, but the epithet most frequently used was dragon. On occasions, both lion and dragon were used as was the case in a contemporary poem addressed by Einion Wan to Dafydd:

Counsel I give to the open-handed ruler of Anglesey,
Generous David of the stock of wise ones;
Let him be liberal, let him be a patron of the bards,
Let him be a lion, let him be a dragon leader.

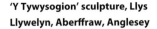

'Y Tywysogion' sculpture, Llys Llywelyn, Aberffraw, Anglesey

The village of Aberffraw upon the island of Anglesey is situated upon the west bank of the river Ffraw. During the mediaeval period, Aberffraw became the traditional court and state capital of the princes of Gwynedd. The only physical evidence that remains of this former epicentre of Welsh royal power is a 12th century Romanesque chancel arch which is housed inside the village church of St Beuno. A sculptured monument dedicated to the princes of Gwynedd was unveiled during 1970 and can be found within the grounds of the village's Llys Llywelyn Heritage Centre.

A 14th century manuscript depiction of King John hunting. Prince Dafydd's mother Joan (Siwan) was the illegitimate daughter of King John of England. Dafydd never knew his English grandfather as John died shortly after Dafydd's birth on 19th of October 1216.

Owain Gwynedd, the great-grandfather of Prince Dafydd (ruled as prince of Gwynedd 1137–70). After his death the royal court at Aberffraw diminished in status, allowing the court at Garth Celyn to then become the all-important and chief residence of the royal families of Gwynedd. (Author's personal photograph of an exhibition panel depicting the Battle of Crogen (1165); panel located at Castle Mill wood, Chirk, near Wrexham.)

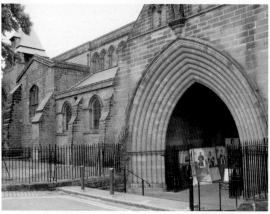

The original Chester Cathedral

During May 1205, Prince Llywelyn the Great married Princess Joan (Siwan), the daughter of King John of England in the historic city of Chester. However, the actual location of the celebrated royal marriage is still open to debate, the principal contenders being the Church of St John the Baptist (the original cathedral), and the present day cathedral (originally the Church of St Peter and St Paul and later the Abbey of St Werburgh). Married by Geoffrey de Muschamp, the serving bishop of Chester, evidence leans towards the older of the two institutions, the 7th century established Church of St John the Baptist as, during the period of the reign of King John, this original cathedral site was considered by all to be the principal religious institution of Chester, therefore being much greater in stature and importance than its near neighbour.

Two Norman lions passant gardant. The coat-of-arms of William the Conqueror and successors, 1066 (left).

Three Plantagenet Lions. The coat-of-arms of Richard the Lionheart and successors, 1198 (right).

Newark Castle, Newark-on-Trent, Nottinghamshire

On the 19th of October 1216, King John of England died at the Midlands castle. Now reduced to a romantic ruin, all that remains of this once mighty fortification is the gatehouse, including chapel and lodgings, the curtain wall and the structure of the west tower.

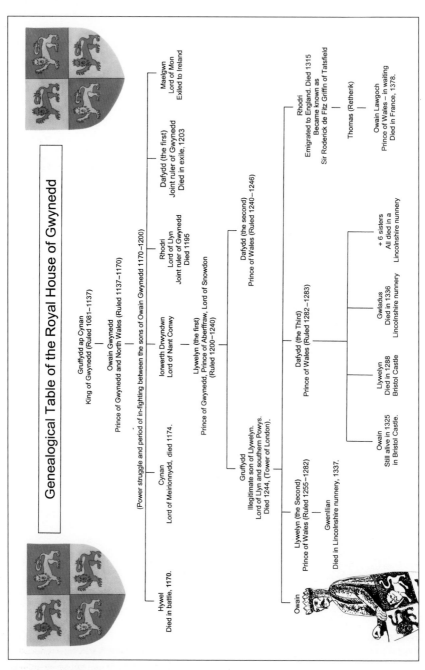

Genealogical Table of the Royal House of Gwynedd

Gruffydd ap Cynan
King of Gwynedd (Ruled 1081–1137)

Owain Gwynedd
Prince of Gwynedd and North Wales (Ruled 1137–1170)

(Power struggle and period of in-fighting between the sons of Owain Gwynedd 1170–1200)

Hywel
Died in battle, 1170.

Cynan
Lord of Meirionnydd, died 1174.

Iorwerth Drwyndwn
Lord of Nant Conwy

Rhodri
Lord of Llyn
Joint ruler of Gwynedd
Died 1195

Dafydd (the first)
Joint ruler of Gwynedd
Died in exile, 1203

Maelgwn
Lord of Mon
Exiled to Ireland

Llywelyn (the first)
Prince of Gwynedd, Prince of Aberffraw, Lord of Snowdon
(Ruled 1200–1240)

Gruffydd
Illegitimate son of Llywelyn.
Lord of Llyn and southern Powys.
Died 1244, (Tower of London).

Dafydd (the second)
Prince of Wales (Ruled 1240–1246)

Llywelyn (the Second)
Prince of Wales (Ruled 1255–1282)

Gwenllian
Died in Lincolnshire nunnery, 1337.

Dafydd (the Third)
Prince of Wales (Ruled 1282–1283)

Rhodri
Emigrated to England. Died 1315
Became known as
Sir Roderick de Fitz Griffin of Tatsfield

Thomas (Retherik)

Owain Lawgoch
Prince of Wales – in waiting
Died in France, 1378.

Owain

Owain
Still alive in 1325
in Bristol Castle.

Llywelyn
Died in 1288
Bristol Castle

Gwladus
Died in 1336
Lincolnshire nunnery

+ 6 sisters
All died in a
Lincolnshire nunnery

Illustration of genealogical table of the royal house of Gwynedd.

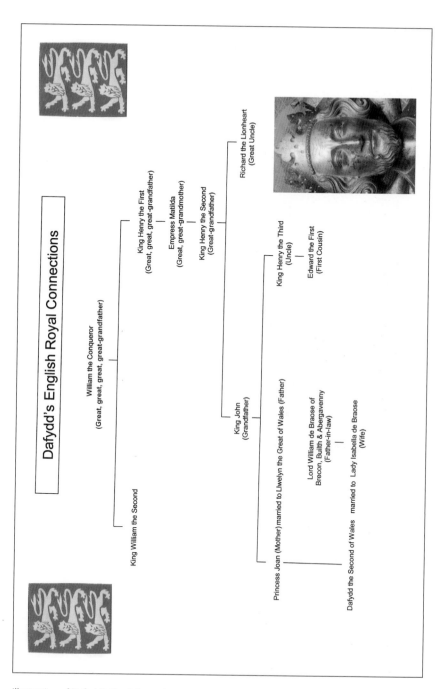

Illustration of Dafydd's English royal connections.

Worcester Cathedral, England

Prince Dafydd's father-in-law, King John of England died on the 19th of October 1216, and his body was taken to Worcester Cathedral where it was elaborately interred. His magnificent tomb and effigy can still be seen amidst the spectacular grandeur of today's cathedral. He became the first English king since Harold Godwinson (c.1020–66) to be born and to die in England.

After his death at Newark Castle in Nottinghamshire, King John was laid to rest inside the precincts of Worcester Cathedral. His tomb effigy can still be seen.

(Author's photograph)

Abergavenny Castle, Gwent

During the year 1175, Abergavenny Castle in Gwent was amongst the prized possessions of William de Braose, the deeply despised Anglo-Norman lord of the district. His position in the hall of infamy was indelibly confirmed by him masterminding the barbarous act that came to be known as the Banquet of Death, to which he successfully lured a group of Gwent noblemen to his Abergavenny castle base where, once trapped inside its walls, they were wantonly butchered by de Braose's heavily armed reception committee.

Coats-of-arms attributed to the Anglo-Norman family of de Braose, a powerful marcher dynasty whose ravenous tentacles cast themselves over considerable areas of middle Wales including Abergavenny, Brecon, Builth and Radnor. William "the ogre of Abergavenny" de Braose (d. 1211) and a later William de Braose (d. 1230), known to the Welsh as 'Black William', were two infamous members drawn from its ranks.

Pen-y-Bryn, Garth Celyn, Abergwyngregyn, Gwynedd

Within the modern-day village of Abergwyngregyn (The Bay of the White Seashells) and only a stone's throw away from the A55 Carriageway between Bangor and Llanfairfechan, there exists a modern-day residence that once belonged to the Welsh princes of Gwynedd. Shortly after the reign of Prince Owain Gwynedd (d. 1170), the princes' chief residence at Aberffraw upon Anglesey diminished in status and the royal residence at Garth Celyn grew in eminence to become the chief residence of the princes and their royal families. At Llys Garth Celyn, we are certain of the occurrence there of one royal birth (Princess Gwenllian, daughter of Llywelyn ap Gruffydd, on the 19th of June 1282) and three royal deaths (Princess Siwan, wife of Llywelyn ap Iorwerth during February 1237; Prince Dafydd ap Llywelyn on the 25th of February 1246 and Princess Eleanor, wife of Llywelyn ap Gruffydd on the 19th of June 1282). At Abergwyngregyn today, there exists a manor house that is dominated by a mediaeval tower. The house that currently occupies the site of Garth Celyn is known as Pen-y-Bryn and the tangible evidence of recent archaeological findings has proved beyond all reasonable doubt that the manor is, in fact, the former royal home or *cartref* of the Welsh princes of 13th century Wales, and although part of the main structure was demolished to create a manor house, the main part of the princes' old home remains intact and has been incorporated into the existing structure.

Hanging Marsh, Garth Celyn

On the 2nd of May 1230, William de Braose was executed at the royal residence of Garth Celyn in Gwynedd. The most shocking of royal scandals materialized when the Anglo-Norman lord was discovered inside Princess Siwan's private chambers. Upon the will and sanction of Prince Llywelyn's royal council, de Braose was indignantly hanged directly above the sewage pit at the royal residence in front of eight hundred of the prince's subjects. The spot is still known today as Gwern y Grog – Hanging Marsh and an existing tree at today's residence of Pen-y-Bryn is said to mark the exact spot where the doomed de Braose was taken and then abruptly dispatched to his death.

Llanfaes, Anglesey

During the 12th and 13th centuries, the important harbour of Llanfaes upon the island of Anglesey was regarded as the chief commercial centre within the kingdom of Gwynedd. Ships laden with cargoes of wine, salt and iron passed through its busy waters and the vibrant mediaeval port also provided its community with a weekly market and an annual trade fair. The Welsh princes oversaw trade links with Ireland and mainland Europe, which proved crucial to help raise taxes to pay for their regular wars against the English crown. The parish of Llanfaes grew further in importance with the establishment of a Franciscan friary, erected there to serve as a sacred burial ground for female members of Welsh royalty. Dafydd's mother, Siwan (d. 1237), and Llywelyn ap Grufffydd's mother, Senana (d. 1263) and wife, Eleanor de Montfort (d. 1282) were all interred there. During the reign of Dafydd ap Llywelyn, Llanfaes formed the

epicentre of Anglesey's important fishing industry, but four decades after his death, Llanfaes dwindled in importance due to the abandonment of the borough by its Welsh citizens, who in their entirety had been forced to resettle at Newborough shortly after the Edwardian conquest. Sadly, there is nothing now that remains of this important historical site, with the exception of some field names and the name of a house which gladly reminds us of its former existence.

Princess Siwan's tomb, Beaumaris Church, Anglesey

In the main porchway of the parish church of St Mary and St Nicholas in the town of Beaumaris upon the isle of Anglesey, there lies the preserved stone coffin that once held the mortal body of Princess Siwan (Joan), wife of Llywelyn the Great and mother to Prince Dafydd. After its removal from its original resting place at the nearby friary of Llanfaes, the coffin was used for many years as a horse watering trough within a local field. Thankfully, the sacred relic has been saved from such criminal indignity and has been relocated within the 14th century established Anglesey church.

Strata Florida Abbey, Pontrhydfendigaid, Dyfed

During October 1238, a meticulously organised national assembly involving all the princes and magnates of Wales took place at the Cistercian abbey of Strata Florida in Dyfed. The nobles who attended were each required to swear an oath of fealty to Llywelyn's youngest born son and elected heir-apparent, Dafydd. There is a possibility that the national convention could in fact have served the purpose of being the public investiture of Dafydd as ruling prince, as at this stage of Llywelyn's life, the ageing prince was deemed to be suffering from the detrimental effects of ill-health. The abbey of Strata Florida (translated as Vale of Flowers) was founded in June 1164 by the Norman baron, Robert Fitz Stephen. However, the ruling Welsh prince of Deheubarth, the Lord Rhys ap Gruffydd successfully overran Fitz Stephen's estates and from that time onwards the religious settlement became a cherished and important centre for Welsh culture and influence. It is believed that a large portion of the ancient manuscript known as *Brut y Tywysogion* (The Chronicle of the Princes) was compiled at this important religious site.

Aberconwy Abbey, 11th April 1240. Llywelyn the Great upon his death bed, attended by his two sons Dafydd and Gruffydd. (Redrawn from the 13th century chronicle of Matthew Paris.)

Maenan Abbey, near Llanrwst, Gwynedd

During the year 1283, the abbey of Aberconwy – burial place of the Welsh princes – was demolished upon the orders of King Edward the First of England, the eventual conqueror of Wales. In its place began the large scale construction of Conwy Castle. All of the precious relics, including the sacred tombs containing the bodies of Welsh royalty, were subsequently rehoused some ten miles downstream at the fledgling abbey of Maenan. However, some three centuries later, the life cycle of that abbey was also terminated, this time as a result of the dissolution of the monasteries during the year 1538. Although the stone coffin of Prince Llywelyn the Great ingeniously survived the savagery of the countrywide cull, the fate of the individual sarcophaguses that once held the remains of his two sons was not as fortunate and rather sadly they vanished from public view as a result of either damage or deliberate destruction.

Gwydir Chapel, Llanrwst, Gwynedd

Gwydir Chapel in the centre of Llanrwst has become the third and final venue for the stone sarcophagus which once held the mortal remains of Prince Llywelyn the Great. Originally placed inside the abbey of Aberconwy, the great man's tomb was subsequently moved to the safety of nearby Maenan Abbey upon Aberconwy's demolition. Eventually, the coffin arrived at its final resting place inside the chapel of Gwydir in Llanrwst. At the time of Llywelyn's burial, his stone tomb would have formed a truly magnificent spectacle as it would have been beautifully adorned with a glittering array of fitted jewels of all descriptions, including sapphires, emeralds and rubies. The royal tombs of his two sons, Gruffydd and Dafydd, would not have been too dissimilar in appearance to that of the father's.

Bangor Cathedral, Gwynedd

Bangor can lay claim to being the oldest cathedral upon the British Isles and was originally founded during or around the year 546 AD. During the summer of 1240, Richard, the serving bishop of Bangor, resigned his position after Prince Dafydd had deliberately enlisted the unsuspecting bishop during his successful initiative that manufactured the arrest and detention

of his elder brother and chief opponent, Gruffydd. Apparently oblivious to the cunning Dafydd's orchestrated plot, the enraged bishop resigned his position rather than continue to serve a prince who favoured deceit. However, during the following year of Dafydd's reign, Richard returned to his exalted position to once again serve as bishop of the diocese.

Cricieth Castle

Built by Llywelyn ap Iorwerth sometime during the 1230s, the stone-built castle that impressively crowns a rocky peninsula overlooking Tremadog Bay was inherited by Prince Dafydd upon the death of his father. The castle formed the prison quarters of the Lord Gruffydd, Llywelyn's eldest son and Dafydd's wayward brother, who was imprisoned there in 1240, where he languished for a spell before being released upon the orders of King Henry the Third.

Dolwyddelan Castle, near Blaenau Ffestiniog, Gwynedd

Overlooking the Lledr valley in the heart of Snowdonia, the eye-catching ruin of Dolwyddelan Castle has successfully maintained its dominating position upon the summit of an accommodating rocky hill. After the death of its founder, Llywelyn ap Iorwerth, the stone fortification, which must have formed a truly impressive spectacle during its heyday – came into the inherited possession of his son, Dafydd.

Maes Mynan, near Caerwys, Clwyd

Throughout the 12th and 13th centuries, a Welsh royal residence belonging to the princes of Gwynedd stood near to the historic hamlet of Caerwys in north-central Flintshire. The former royal court of Maes Mynan, sometimes referred to in contemporary manuscripts as Aber-Chwiler, was situated near to the modern day nursing home of Maes Mynan Hall in Afonwen. Sadly, all visible traces of the ancient royal enclosure have been destroyed, largely due to the efforts of the local quarry industry.

Cymer Abbey, Dolgellau, Gwynedd

Founded during the latter part of the 12th century, the Cistercian abbey of Cymer, near Dolgellau in Gwynedd became an important component in the machinery of the Welsh state. By keeping, copying and recording vital documents of national interest, religious institutions such as Cymer earned for themselves the loyalty and trust of their royal masters. At Cymer, the resident monks also maintained a notable stud, providing high-quality horses to the service of Prince Llywelyn ap Iorwerth. We must therefore assume that the provision to Welsh royalty of this pedigree of steeds would have continued into the reign of Llywelyn's successor, Dafydd.

Carndochan Castle, near Bala

Built by the Welsh princes of Gwynedd during the first part of the 13th century, there is now little that remains of this stone structure. Only mounds of collapsed stone, and some exposed wall-faces are still visible on the wind-battered ridge.

Castell-y-Bere, near Dolgellau, Gwynedd
Located in the foothills of Cadair Idris in the upper Dysynni valley, the castle of Y Bere is the largest of the native strongholds of northern Wales and it was only built as a direct consequence of a dispute between Llywelyn the Great and his eldest son, Gruffydd. Gruffydd had previously been granted the territorial rights over Ardudwy and Meirionnydd in north-west Wales, but his fiery ambition still caused him to rebel against his father. During the subsequent crisis of 1221, war was averted and having dispossessed his son of the district (*cantref*) of Meirionnydd, Llywelyn built the castle of Y Bere to safeguard his power in that domain.

Llys Rhosyr, Newborough, Anglesey
The royal court at Rhosyr was regularly used by the princes of Gwynedd until the culmination of the Edwardian Conquest in 1283. The *llys* at Rhosyr remains the only royal court of the princes of Gwynedd of which the ground plan survives almost intact.

St Peter's Church, Newborough, Anglesey
The church of St Peter in Newborough – originally dedicated to St Ano and later St Mary – once served the royal court of the Welsh princes at nearby Rhosyr. The church is regarded as being the longest in length upon the island of Anglesey and a large section of the present day structure has miraculously survived from the period of the native princes, including the font and nave.

Dolbadarn Castle, Llanberis, Gwynedd
The castle of Dolbadarn, which is overshadowed by the rugged heights of Snowdonia, was built by Prince Llywelyn ap Iorwerth and upon his death, the stone-built fortress was inherited by his son and successor, Dafydd the Second. The original tower built by Llywelyn remains remarkably preserved and forms a picturesque image against the backdrop of the mist shrouded slopes of Wales' highest peak.

A contemporary image of Dafydd's uncle and adversary, King Henry the Third of England. During his fifty-six year reign, the English monarch launched more military campaigns against Wales, ten in all, than any other English sovereign before or after.

Ewloe Castle, Flintshire

It is believed that Llywelyn ap Iorwerth was responsible for the first phase of construction at the borderlands castle – now reduced to a picturesque and somewhat romantic ruin – and upon his death, the manor of Ewloe passed to his son, Dafydd. The less ruinous of the two surviving towers, known locally as the Welsh Tower, is believed to be an extension attributed to the later period of the reign of Dafydd's nephew, Llywelyn ap Gruffydd.

– I I –

Propelled into the elevated position of elected regent during the course of his father's final years of deteriorating health, Dafydd was stung into action by his elder brother's latest drive for dynastic power. If left unmolested, the seething cauldron of hate that emanated from the hotbed of the Lord Gruffydd's traditional heartlands upon Llŷn would surely bubble out of control and result in anarchy and bloodshed throughout the realm of Gwynedd. Acting beneath the banner of Llywelyn's blessing, Dafydd successfully thwarted the foreseen threat of rebellion by a decisive force of arms – perhaps even surprising his elder brother with the qualities of speed, intensity and aggression that could only be attributed to the character of a worthy and competent warrior. Likewise, the unruly spectral figure of Gruffydd – who being the habitual wreaker of havoc during the period of Llywelyn's lengthy reign – ultimately forced the will of his father into orchestrating one final act of political action. During the October of 1238 and, after many months of intricate preparation, Prince Llywelyn gathered all of the Welsh princes and magnates of Wales at a national assembly inside the Cistercian abbey of Strata Florida in Dyfed, in which all those present swore an oath of allegiance specifically to the young Dafydd. It is more than possible that the historic convention could in fact have formed Dafydd's public investiture as the new Prince of Gwynedd. Moreover, the success of the regal gathering delivered what must have appeared to be a career defining and crushing blow to the ambition of the Lord Gruffydd, and the occurrence of the unprecedented mass gathering effectively reduced his figure to a status not too dissimilar to that of a royal pariah.

On the 11th of April 1240, the curtain finally came down upon the golden episode of Prince Llywelyn's incredible forty year long reign. To every intent and purpose, the recognized Prince of Aberffraw and Lord of Snowdon had, in fact been, during the period of his later lifetime, the undisputed master of Welsh Wales, such was his remarkable success as the pre-eminent Welsh ruler of the period. The day before his capitulation to death, Llywelyn had voluntarily entered the holy precincts of Aberconwy Abbey where, in accordance with the custom of Welsh royalty, he donned the cloth of the monastic habit and there prepared himself to be received by the heavenly father. Inside the abbey church of Aberconwy was where he remained, whereupon the signal of death, the perished sovereign of Gwynedd was afforded the dignified offerings of a royal burial, his body being embalmed in spicery, virgin wax and cumin; and amidst an unfolding pageant of sorrow, glory and honour, he was dutifully interred inside a magnificent jewel encrusted stone sarcophagus which had already been prepared for the "True Lord of the Land". In the wake of the royal death, Dafydd ascended the vacant throne to become Prince Dafydd the Second of Gwynedd.

Dafydd moved rapid in order to protect the precincts of his precious sovereignty, orchestrating one final and determined campaign to forever eradicate the menacing threat caused by the lurking shadow of his ever dangerous half-brother, Gruffydd. Dafydd had already confiscated Gruffydd's hold over Powys, depriving him of all the land assets of the respective territories of Arwystli, Ceri, Cyfeiliog, Mochnant and Caereinion, leaving his bitterly frustrated other-half with the solitary lordship of Llŷn. The decisive moment arrived during the summer of 1240, when Gruffydd received his coup de grace courtesy of a swift manoeuvre delivered by Dafydd. Summoned to attend a peace meeting in the presence of Richard, the serving Bishop of Bangor, Gruffydd and his eldest son, Owen Goch (born c.1219), were particularly anxious to state their case to the trusted corner of a neutral ear. Instead, the unsuspecting Lord of Llŷn fell victim to an act of beguilement during the occasion of what proved to be a dramatic royal rendezvous. Gruffydd and Owen Goch were both arrested upon Dafydd's personal orders and then, without further hesitation, the stunned duo were spirited away to the secure fastness and detention of Cricieth Castle. The serving bishop was understandably enraged by the occurrence of the ruse and, being personally oblivious to Dafydd's cunning scheme, the churchman immediately resigned his exalted position rather than him serve a deceitful prince. If the supreme council of Gwynedd were also unaware of the contents of the masterly plot, complain they did not after its successful execution. Dafydd now stood victorious as the solitary heir and successor. He had gladly inherited a unique chain of fortifications that circumnavigated the realm, including such structures as Carndochan (near Bala), Carn Fadryn, Aber-Ia, Castell-y-Bere, Cricieth, Deganwy, Dolbadarn, Dolwyddelan and Ewloe; and also, he had acquired the abundant use of an effective quantum of established royal courts or *llysoedd*, which included those at Rhosyr, Cemaes, and Aberffraw upon the island of Anglesey, and elsewhere at Abergwyngregyn, Trefriw, Maes Mynan, Ystumgwern and Coleshill. Dafydd also inherited his father's *teulu*, as during the mediaeval age every Welsh prince – including those of lesser dynasties – possessed a *teulu*. The term *teulu* can best be described as meaning royal bodyguard, household troop or even war-band. The principal function of such an important body was the protection of the royal master, about whom it was to be found at all times. If contemporary estimates are to be believed, the Welsh princes had at their command a *teulu* of around 120 to 150 men.

However, Dafydd quickly discovered that the transition from temporary regent of Gwynedd to the position of permanent ruler would be anything other than a clearly defined and ripple-free passage. Barely one month after the death of his father and the subsequent glory of his own elevation to power, the new prince of Gwynedd was summoned to appear before the royal court of King Henry the Third of England at Gloucester. On the 15th of May 1240, the suffocating terms that had been inscribed within the fabric of the Treaty of Gloucester not only severely dented the ego of the seemingly confident Dafydd, but crucially they also derailed any immediate hopes that the ambitious young prince harboured of attempting to emulate his father's previous great deeds.

Dafydd was forced to officially recognise his royal uncle, King Henry the Third of England, as his feudal superior and, furthermore, he was consigned to a position where he must personally pledge himself as a liegeman of the king of England. Moreover, Henry specifically humiliated the inexperienced Welsh prince further by refusing to consider or even acknowledge his official royal title, instead coolly referring to him only as "son of Llywelyn, sometime Prince of Aberffraw and Lord of Gwynedd". During the occasion of the state ceremony held at Gloucester, Dafydd would have presented himself as a dignified spectacle at the head of the invited Welsh delegation. How English eyes must have purposely strained for the benefit of that very first curious glimpse of Gwynedd's new prince. Standing tall, immaculately dressed in the finery of tailor-made royal robes fittingly adorned with the recognized insignia of his princedom, a sheathed sword at his belt and wearing proudly the glittering gold circlet crown of Gwynedd upon his young head, Dafydd, accompanied by his chosen royal entourage from Wales, must have strode into the assembled seminar at Gloucester with an air of optimism and confidence. Instead, the humiliating content of the treaty seemingly served only to demean in status such royal regalia traditionally worn on listed occasions of state such as at Gloucester as dynastic artefacts possessed by nothing other than an insignificant and lame-spirited serfdom.

In the wake of the Treaty of Gloucester, the demoralised Dafydd endured a ceaseless cycle of turbulence from every source imaginable. In the eyes of King Henry, Dafydd's considered sphere of influence was to be solely consigned to the domain of Gwynedd with no legal right to the manifestation of a wider and greater lordship. Likewise, King Henry began to exert further pressure upon the young Dafydd's shoulders when he directly challenged the Prince of Gwynedd's so-called hereditary claim to the respective territories of Builth, southern Powys and Cardigan. The escalating crisis deepened for Dafydd when a number of influential Welsh magnates formerly loyal to the rule of his father decidedly deserted him during his impending hour of need. As the swooping vultures excitedly eyed their prey, the carcass of Dafydd's ever increasing vulnerability was further exposed when the *cantref* of Maeliennydd in central Wales was restored to Ralph Mortimer; the manor of Kinnerly returned to the jurisdiction of its former lord and the commote of Penmaen in Gower changed hands. The principality that Dafydd had only recently inherited threatened to shrink further in size when lawsuits were delivered against the respective lordships of Mold and Bromfield in north-east Wales. Furthermore, many of Dafydd's Welsh tenants in Gwynedd were aggrieved at the hostile nature surrounding the capture, imprisonment and subsequent disinheritance suffered by his brother, Gruffydd. As the gravity of immense pressure bore down upon his heavily burdened shoulders, Dafydd chose wisely to submit all of the impeded lands in question to the jurisdiction of a council of arbitrators, who were to be nominated by the fair will of both sides. Embroiled within the fierce grip of crisis, Dafydd skillfully evaded an outcome by choosing to deliberately delay the legal process for more than one full year in length. The result of Dafydd's defiant refusal to conform simply detonated King Henry's simmering rage into a mood of total fury, worse so when Dafydd steadfastly refused all requests to release the brother that he so despised from the restraint of captivity. As the unfolding drama deepened, Dafydd turned to desperate measures by attempting to enlist the foreign support of the royal court of King Louis IX of France. However, the bold jaunt to the foreign shores was destined for both disappointment and failure. Dafydd now stood alone to incur the expected wrath of the English king. King Henry the Third of England was not an opponent one could easily sweep aside and the pages of Welsh history duly testify that during a subsequent reign that spanned a total of fifty-six years in length (1216–72), he launched more military campaigns against Wales – ten in all – than any other English king before or after. The die for conflict had been firmly cast.

During August 1241, the overwhelming might of the menacing English war machine came bearing down upon the northern lands of Wales. From their assembled base at Shrewsbury, King Henry led a great force of men northwards towards the border city of Chester; from there they would march across the compliant fords of the Dee river in order to penetrate the exposed membrane of Prince Dafydd's fragile realm. The Welsh weather, which during previous conflicts had so often proved to be the trusted and mischievous tormentor of invading English armies, was strangely subservient during the occasion of the warm, dry summer of 1241, and the havoc typically associated with the regular fiendish elements of Welsh weather conditions was nonexistent, even surprising Henry's advancing soldiery who were to become blessed by the most favourable of conditions. There had been no incessant rainfall since the time of spring and the once gushing rivers of the northern terrain had duly surrendered to the overwhelming power of the prickly heat – and most had sunk meekly into their beds. Elsewhere, deep pools of water had completely dried up to leave nothing but a visible grey residue of cracked earthen craters; even the hazardous bogs and swampy marsh lands – now transformed into dry, negotiable plains – had fallen victim to the curse of the drought. Unimpeded, the English war machine powered onwards like an unstoppable juggernaut. Conquering the densely wooded forests of Tegeingl, they clattered westwards in search of the summer lanes to Rhuddlan, a colourful column of moving men, a dazzling and awe inducing spectacle and one in methodical pursuit of action, new adventure and triumph. King Henry had brought with his host a mighty phalanx of conscripted soldiers, men-at-arms, companies of trained archers and the proud lords who rode high on their caparisoned horses. The archers were regarded as a formidable force amidst the ranks of any mediaeval army and this elite special force could unleash a devastating holocaust upon any enemy unfortunate to stand in its path. It has been estimated that during the course of one minute, a single mediaeval archer could loose 12 arrows against a range of 250 yards. Therefore, a drilled company of 100 firing men could accurately deliver an astonishing deluge of up to 1,200 arrows per minute, such was the effectiveness of the mediaeval age's very own "weapon of mass destruction".

Prior to the implementation of hostilities against Dafydd, King Henry had agreed a pact with the wife of the incarcerated Gruffydd ap Llywelyn who, during this period, was still being held under armed guard within the constrictive confines of Cricieth Castle. Anxious to highlight the plight of her husband and his subsequent fall from grace, Lady Senana had succeeded in courting the intervention of English royal assistance in the ongoing quest for the achievement of Gruffydd's release. Anticipating an English battlefield triumph against the heavily out-numbered Dafydd, the plucky Senana had timed her initiative to perfection. Any well-meaning assurances received from the bosom of the English royal court during the build-up to the impending conflict would trustingly lead to the liberation of her husband, the eldest born son of Llywelyn. The treaty between Henry and Senana was formulated in Shrewsbury, the town of the king's muster on the 12th of August 1241, and was undersigned with the respective pledges of Lord Roger Montalt of Mold, Ralph Mortimer, Walter Clifford, Lord Gruffydd ap Madog of Bromfield and Gruffydd ap Gwenwynwyn of southern Powys. From every avenue conceivable, Dafydd – now isolated and newly exposed to the prospect of defeat and ruin – faced a growing concoction of powerful enemies who had all united in the mission to deliver Dafydd's downfall.

The inevitable English triumph arrived via a lightning campaign that lasted less than a fortnight in duration. Glaringly exposed in the unforgiving theatre of war by the more experienced Henry, Dafydd was rendered shell-shocked by the sheer speed and rapid fluidity of Henry's forceful advancement into the Vale of Clwyd. Dafydd's vulnerability was further exposed by the fact that he had naively neglected to maintain a crucial lifeline link to the mountainous region of Snowdonia – a natural citadel that his forces of defence could have readily occupied as a final avenue of resistance. In real terms, how could the overstretched Dafydd have ever hoped to have won a conflict in which the considerable gulf of numbers between the opposing camp of his many enemies and that of his precious few allies was so vast. On the 29th of August 1241, Dafydd decidedly sought terms of peace at a place called Gwern Eigron, near

Llanelwy (St Asaph) in the Vale of Clwyd. The bloodless call to arms was over. Dafydd's humiliation was confirmed the following morning when amidst the thunder of galloping hooves, Dafydd, accompanied by a small band of trusted delegates, rode into the tented field headquarters of his victorious royal uncle at Rhuddlan. Whilst kneeling upon the parched earth outside the king's tent, the humbled figure of Dafydd heard first-hand the humiliating terms of the peace. The wounding substance employed by the respective treaties of Gwern Eigron (29 August 1241) and Rhuddlan (30 and 31 August 1241) dehydrated Dafydd of all his power. The lordship of Mold in north-east Wales was officially ceded to the Anglo Norman family of Montalt, the Welsh *cantref* (district) of Meirionnydd in north-west Wales was returned to the sons of Meredith and the northern lands of Tegeingl, Ellesmere and Deganwy were all transferred into the hands of the English crown. The misery of defeat was amplified by the painful fact that Dafydd was ordered to compensate Henry his entire war expenses. Furthermore, the lands of southern Powys reverted to Gruffydd ap Gwenwynwyn and the freshly defeated prince of Gwynedd was ordered to release his much feared brother, Gruffydd, into the care of the English royal court. Moreover, the golden empire that his father Prince Llywelyn had proudly presided over had rapidly diminished after the short period of only one dry summer, its new figurehead, Dafydd, tragically reduced to the subdued position of a toothless tribal chieftain.

The Lord Gruffydd, freshly liberated from the restraints of his incarceration at Cricieth, was courteously welcomed at the London court of the victorious King Henry. Whilst lodged within the confines of accommodating quarters inside the high keep at the Tower of London, Gruffydd patiently awaited the prospect of his eventual release. However, growing increasingly restless from the monotony of the many long days spent inside the isolation of the Tower, Gruffydd was gradually confronted with the harsh reality of his own situation. His own children could come and go as they freely pleased, within the royal complex, as could his wife, the Lady Senana, but Gruffydd's individual freedom of movement was specifically restricted to the immediate area of his own provided quarters.

When the long, dry season of summer surrendered to the advent of autumn, Gruffydd dejectedly resigned himself to the cruel hand that fate had dealt him, and reluctantly, he was forced to concede to his new position as King Henry's political pawn. Relishing his devious role as puppet master, Henry contentedly licked his lips at the prospect of holding both of the sons of the legendary Llywelyn to ransom. Maintaining Gruffydd in the secure confinement of English royal custody, who for so long had proved to be the hovering spectral figure that formed Dafydd's Achilles heel, would knowingly implant fear and paranoia into the psyche of the vastly reduced Dafydd; whilst the long suffering Gruffydd had merely swapped the cramped quarters of a prison cell in Wales to one as equally restrictive in neighbouring England. Not for the first time, nor would this prove to be the last occasion, would a ruling sovereign of England devoutly choose to embrace the proven adage that, "A kingdom divided against itself will always fall to ruin and defeat".

On the 24th of October 1241, Dafydd, at the head of his mounted entourage, clattered through the imposing gates of entry of that very same city which still harboured his brother. The prince had been summoned from Gwynedd to attend Westminster, the nerve centre of English royal power. The Hall there was begun by King William the Second of England (William Rufus – The Red, reigned 1087–1100) during the 1090s and at the time it was the largest hall in England. Since the period of its construction, successive English monarchs had used the lavishly decorated hall for ceremonial occasions such as coronation banquets and lyings-in-state. Entering the interior of the hall that hosted Henry's royal court, Dafydd's wholesale submission to the sovereign of England was confirmed in the form of one final compliant act of homage. As Dafydd ceremoniously sank to his knees upon the hard symmetrically tiled floor of the chamber in full view of the king's assembled royal council, his conqueror had submitted one further clause to the volume of the existing treaty of peace signed at Rhuddlan. It read, "Notification that, should he (Dafydd) die without a legitimate heir, he grants, of his own free will, all the lands of the principality of north Wales to the King and his heirs, so that they may succeed him in all that land for ever, and orders all his men and subjects to obey the King and his heirs as their true lords if that should happen." Without complaint or even a single word of princely protest, Dafydd dutifully bound the treaty with the authority of his personal seal. It was now a legal binding document.

Maintaining Gruffydd ap Llywelyn hostage and depriving him of any realistic hope of release had proved to be a worthwhile enterprise of Henry's cunning. Locked away within the claustrophobic confines of the Tower of London, Dafydd was only too aware that the isolated, but ever dangerous figure of his brother could, at any given moment of Henry's choosing be used to spearhead a renewed challenge against his rule in Gwynedd. However, the firm stranglehold that Henry held over Dafydd was vanquished forever when news of a dramatic event at the Tower of London filtered through the walls of the Welsh royal court of Gwynedd to reach the shocked ears of all those who resided within. During the final weeks of February 1244, the cold element of winter had not yet truly subsided in the precincts of east London, so much so that the Lord Gruffydd's personal request to the Tower authorities for extra blankets to be delivered to his cell proved successful, the daily heat from the roaring fire located inside his accommodation seemingly insufficient to warm the ostracized prince. Without drawing suspicion, Gruffydd decidedly chose the precise evening of the 1st of March, St David's Day, during the same year, to enact the most daring of escape ventures from the restrictive private hell that was his prison cell. By using his bed sheets as a make-shift rope, Gruffydd, under the cover of darkness, scrambled from the window space of his lofty prison apartment to begin a calculated bid for freedom. However, tragedy was to befall the hapless Gruffydd when, during the process of his dangerous descent to liberty, the overtaxed vine of linen snapped causing the doomed Gruffydd to hurtle uncontrollably towards the journey of his early death. His broken, blood-stained body was discovered the following morning by shocked Tower guards, his broad neck driven deep into the cavity of his shoulder blades. The misery of Gruffydd's stop-start career was finally over in the most tragic of circumstances. The royal misfit had endured an incredible sixteen years or so of his forty-eight year life as an incarcerated political prisoner of the state, moving in a nomadic fashion from one spell of incarceration to another: Cricieth, Deganwy and London all tainted by his unruly presence. The actual window in which Gruffydd exited for his daring escape attempt can still be seen to this day. The window faces the Traitor's Gate and is located high up on the south-west of the tower at the western end of the Chapel. It would be another four years before the body of the fallen prince was to be returned to Wales for the privilege of a dignified burial, fittingly laid to rest alongside the decorated tomb of his father, Prince Llywelyn, inside the royal abbey church of Aberconwy.

During the period following Gruffydd's catastrophic death at the Tower of London, a disappointed Henry was forced to concede that his recent domineering hold over Dafydd had been vanquished forever. Naturally so, the resounding shockwaves that accompanied the news of the royal death reverberated throughout the lands of Wales. Dafydd, his hands shackled free of all restraint, underwent a revolutionary transformation. Within nine weeks of his brother's death, Dafydd had confidently secured crucial alliances with the majority of the lesser Welsh princes, the chief exceptions being Gruffydd ap Gwenwynwyn of southern Powys and Gruffydd ap Madog, the lord of Bromfield in north-east Wales. Undeniably, Dafydd was now the masterly focus of all Welsh discontent, even more so when a sizeable proportion of his old foes, including those that once belonged to his brother's retinue, willingly pledged their solidarity with the growing ambition of Llywelyn's one remaining son. Patriotism – during any given time, in any given country – grows strongest when it is fertilized by military success and Dafydd's halcyon period of triumph was fast approaching.

During June 1244, marauding bands of mounted Welsh guerilla fighters began to plunder English-held estates throughout the Marcher lands, deliberately conducting a series of daring raids carried out beneath the protective blanket of nightfall. By expanding the field operations, the revitalized Dafydd thundered southwards with his armed force, invading the *cantref* (district) of Cyfeiliog in Powys, the lordship of his principal Welsh enemy, Gruffydd ap Gwenwynwyn, the prince of Powys Wenwynwyn (southern Powys). Unimpressed by the procedure of Dafydd's recent charm offensive, the defiant Powysian prince had flatly refused to honour Dafydd's ambitious drive to become the dominant leader in Welsh Wales. Unfortunately for Gruffydd, as the hereditary leader of a Welsh princedom with vulnerable and often hostile borders, he had naturally inherited the age-old problem of allegiance. Walking a political tightrope – just as his father and grandfather before him had to, he could choose to either pledge his support towards the corner of the princes of Gwynedd who were based upon his northern frontier, or alternatively he could offer it to the opposing corner of the kings of England whose territories hugged the eastern flank of his realm. Gruffydd chose England. Finding the rebellious prince of southern Powys holed up inside his manorial castle of Tafolwern, a short distance to the east of Machynlleth, Dafydd, intent on gaining the hand of Gruffydd's submission, began to lay vigorous siege to the fortified structure. Built upon a parcel of land and protected by a natural barrier of two converging rivers, the castle defended by Gruffydd initially held firm. However, Gruffydd's urgent requests for the intervention of English military assistance had seemingly fallen upon deaf ears, and just prior to Dafydd's successful taking of the castle, the Powysian prince removed himself from the scene and fled to a safer environment. Freshly uniting Wales beneath the canopy of his illuminating leadership, the reincarnated Prince of Gwynedd expanded his campaign and ambitiously sought the aid of European allies. During this frenzied period of activity and rampage, the summer season of 1244 became even more historic when, a body of Dafydd's elected Welsh envoys, were dispatched overseas to visit the Lateran court of Pope Innocent the Fourth in order to appeal on behalf of their prince for the support of the holiest man on Christian Earth. Dafydd had formed the opinion that his policy of open aggression – to which he had enthusiastically embraced – could in fact form a trusted bed partner to political diplomacy, both of which could be utilised as effective weapons during the occasion of Dafydd's renewed struggle with Henry.

Dafydd's groundbreaking directive to secure papal support initially proved fruitful, as the Pontiff's refreshingly worded reply appeared to lean most favourably with the cause of Wales. Dafydd's elected envoys had submitted a selected list of Welsh grievances against King Henry the Third of England, and it was the expressed opinion of the Welsh royal court that the binding treaties that Dafydd had previously agreed with Henry had in fact each been manufactured whilst the Welsh prince was under the strain of duress, and as such they should be declared corrupt and invalid. In response, the Pope issued a written mandate from the Italian papal port city of Genoa. Dated on the 26th of July 1244, and addressed to the chief abbots of the Welsh Cistercian establishments of Aberconwy and Cymer, Pope Innocent the Fourth (previously Bishop Sinibaldo de'Fieschi) ordered the said abbots to conduct an official enquiry concerning the issue of King Henry's political hold over Gwynedd. The King of England was summoned to appear in person before a special hearing that was scheduled to be held at the location of the Clwydian church of Caerwys, near Holywell (Treffynnon) to respond to the deposited Welsh grievances. Furthermore, Dafydd boldy attempted to revolutionise Wales' standing in the greater European theatre. The Prince of Gwynedd proposed to the Pope that Wales be accepted as an official papal dominion – which, if endorsed, would effectively result in the legal castration of all English overlordship absolute. From the despairing doldrums of hopelessness, the charismatic Dafydd had ingeniously revived the hopes and fortunes of his principality. From the ashes of Gwern Eigron the phoenix had undoubtedly arisen. As the crisis rumbled on into a new year and the Welsh raids continued incessant, King Henry empowered a ministerial delegation that included such English heavyweights as John le Strange and Henry of Audley to seek a truce with the resilient Dafydd. However, beginning on the 8th of January 1245, the ongoing negotiations would prove themselves to be futile as both camps markedly embarked upon a menacing route that could only result in further collision and all-out war. For the first time during his short, but turbulent reign, Dafydd began to use the title of Prince of Wales – *Princeps Wallie*. And in doing so, he became the first Welshman in history to ever style himself as such. For his part, and to no one's great surprise, Henry failed to appear for the scheduled hearing at Caerwys, and only a few weeks later, the effluence of diplomacy finally came to a halt to be replaced by a tide of destruction.

Basingwerk Abbey, Greenfield Valley, near Holywell

On the 25th of July, during the year 1240, Prince Dafydd issued his very first charter as the ruling prince of Gwynedd. The historic charter was issued from the very scene of his birthplace, Castell Hen Blas in Coleshill, Flintshire, and its terms awarded the resident Cistercian monks of nearby Basingwerk Abbey full ownership and unhindered jurisdiction over their immediate lands which included mills, farm buildings, pastures, fisheries and a grange. In all, some fifteen Cistercian houses were established in Wales, more than any other order, and of these, eight owed their foundation to Welsh princes.

Dafydd ap Llywelyn's Charter concerning the Abbey of Basingwerk

Original text in Latin, translated as follows:

Grant and confirmation, for the love of God and the salvation of the souls of himself and his father Llywelyn and his mother Joan and all his heirs, in pure and perpetual alms, of all the gifts and liberties which his father Llywelyn and his other predecessors granted to the monastery to be held for ever, free of all earthly service and secular exaction, as freely as any other alms, with all their appurtenances as set out in the present document: namely, the site of the abbey with the mills before the gate: the land before the gates given by Ranulf and his brother Eneas; the land which Maredudd Wawor had in and outside the township of Holywell and the land which his brother, Uchdryd (?) (Huttredus) exchanged in the same township for his share of land in Whitford; the grange of Fulbrook with all its appurtenances and easements and the common pasture of the mountains; the church of Holywell with the chapel of Coleshill and all its appurtenances, so that the monks may have them for their own use for ever; the land and the pasture of Gelli given by his father with all its appurtenances and easements as set out more fully in the charter concerning these. A quitclaims for ever of toll throughout his land and sea on all the monks' sales and purchases. A further grant of two thirds of the tithes of fish caught in the fisheries of Rhuddlan together with the tithe of his share of the fish; the whole of Gwernhefin with all the men of that township and its appurtenances, granted by Owain Brogyntyn; Elise's confirmation of that gift; the lands and pastures of Penllyn given by his father Llywelyn, as set out in the latter's charter. Dafydd and his heirs will warrant all the aforesaid tenements to the monks against all men for ever. Sealing clause; witnesses. Coleshill, 25th July, 1240.

Edeneweth Vakan
Ennio Vakan
Hugone Episco de Sancto Assaf
Gronou filio Kenewreik
Magistro David tunc Cancellario
Heylin' filio Kenrith'
Ph(ilipp)o filio Ywor
Madoc filio Purewenn'

Source: *The Acts of Welsh Rulers 1120–1283*. Edited by Huw Pryce (page 460)

Chester Castle, Cheshire, England

The construction of this important border fortress began sometime around the year 1070 and the project was masterminded by the area's newly installed Norman earl, Hugh "The Wolf" Lupus. Throughout the mediaeval period, Chester Castle was regularly used as a supply base and launch pad for the many military campaigns undertaken by English royalty against northern Wales, including the occasion of Henry the Third's two wars against Dafydd (1241 and 1244–6). The castle was also used as a prison, quickly gaining the reputation of being one of the coldest and most inhumane detention centres throughout mediaeval Britain. Various members of Welsh royalty were incarcerated there, including Owen Goch (eldest son of Gruffydd ap Llywelyn) who was kept there for a period during the war of 1244–6.

Twt Hill Castle / Rhuddlan Castle, Clwyd

Rhuddlan was once the location of the fortified royal court of Gruffydd ap Llywelyn (King of Gwynedd from 1039 and also King of all Wales until his death in 1063). After the Welshman's death, his abandoned royal court – now known locally as Twt Hill – came into the needy hands of Norman lord, Robert of Rhuddlan, a trusted adherent to William the Conqueror. Some two centuries later, King Edward the First completed a second fortress, almost 300 yards to the north of the original. On the 29th of August 1241, Prince Dafydd surrendered at the nearby location of Gwerneigron, and upon the following day inside King Henry's tented battle headquarters at Rhuddlan, the defeated Dafydd was forced to endure the terms of the peace.

Senana's agreement with
King Henry the Third Shrewsbury, 1241

Agreement between the king on one side and Senana, wife of Gruffudd ap
Llywelyn – whom his brother Dafydd holds in prison – together with her son
Owain, on the other: Senana undertakes on behalf of Gruffudd to give the
king 600 marks to free Gruffudd and his son Owain, so that it shall be judged
in the king's court whether he should be imprisoned, and that there after the
king's court shall make a judgement for him and his heirs according to Welsh
law concerning their portion of the patrimony of Llywelyn, Gruffudd's father,
which Dafydd has withheld from Gruffudd. If Gruffudd and his heirs recover
by the judgement of the king's court the portion that they say is theirs of the
aforesaid patrimony. Senana undertakes on behalf of Gruffudd and his heirs that
they shall pay 300 marks per annum for it to the king and his heirs, namely one
third in coin, one third in oxen and cattle, and one third in horses according to
the valuation of lawful men, to be handed over at Shrewsbury to the sheriff of
Shropshire, and by him to the royal exchequer, namely one half at Michaelmas
and the other at Easter. Senana also undertakes on behalf of Gruffudd and
his heirs that they will maintain a firm peace with Dafydd concerning the
portion remaining to Dafydd of the said patrimony; and that if any Welsh
rebel against the king or his heirs, Gruffudd and his heirs will compel them to
make satisfaction. To ensure that all the above terms are observed Senana will
give the king her sons Dafydd and Rhodri as hostages, on condition that if
Gruffudd and 0wain should die before they are released, one of the aforesaid
sons of Senana shall be restored to her. Senana has sworn on the Gospels on
behalf of herself and Gruffudd and his heirs that they will observe all these
terms, and has undertaken that Gruffudd will swear the same when he has
been released. She has submitted herself in Gruffudd's name concerning the
above to the jurisdiction of the bishops of Hereford arid Coventry; so that the
bishops, at the king's request. shall force them to observe all the terms through
excommunication and interdict. Senana has undertaken to ensure that all the
terms are implemented and that, after his release, Gruffudd and his heirs will
confirm them and give their written instrument to the king in the aforesaid
terms. This document has been drawn up as further security, so that Senana has
affixed her husband's seal on the part remaining with the king and the king's seal
has been affixed on the part remaining with her. Senana has given the following
pledges in Gruffudd's name: Ralph Mortimer, Walter Clifford, Roger of Mold,
seneschal of Chester, Maelgwn ap Maelgwn, Maredudd ap Rhobert, Gruffudd
ap Madog of Bromfield and his brothers Hywel and Maredudd and Gruffudd ap
Gwenwynwyn; these have undertaken all the above terms on Senana's behalf
and given their charters to the king concerning them.

Shrewsbury, 12th August 1241

Source: *The Acts of Welsh Rulers 1120–1283*. Edited by Huw Pryce

King Henry's route into Wales, August 1241

Aberffraw

Garth Celyn

Conwy

Cricieth

1. Shrewsbury, August 8th 1241: King Henry begins to gather his troops in preparation for an all-out assault against Dafydd in northern Wales. (On the 12th of August 1241, Senana, wife of Dafydd's brother, Gruffudd, met the king at Shrewsbury to parley on behalf of her imprisoned husband.)

2. Chester, August 24th 1241: King Henry crosses the border into Wales in order to engage Dafydd's army of defence.

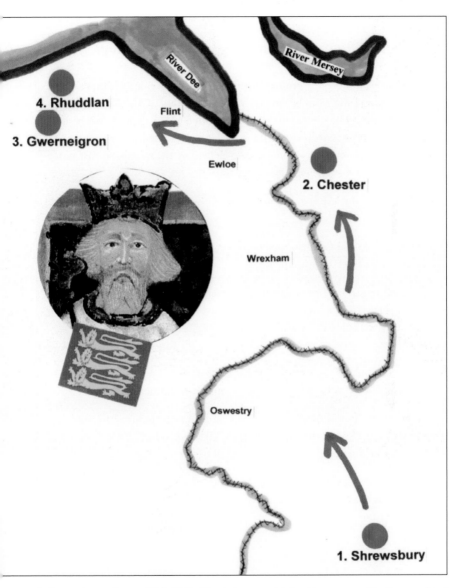

3. Gwerneigron, August 29th 1241: After being completely outmanoeuvred by the speed and fluidity of Henry's troop advancement, Dafydd is forced to sue for peace.

4. Rhuddlan, August 30th-31st 1241: A defeated Dafydd is summoned to appear at Henry's battlecamp, where for two consecutive days his victorious uncle delivers to him the humiliating terms for the peace.

The Peace accord of Gwerneigron, 1241

Notification that he has granted to the king:

1. He will hand over his brother Gruffudd, together with the latter's eldest son and others whom he has imprisoned, to the king and afterwards accept the judgement of the king's court regarding whether Gruffudd should be held captive and whether any portion of the land held by his father Llywelyn ought to pertain to Gruffudd according to the custom of the Welsh, so that peace may be held between Dafydd and Gruffudd.

2. Security for the maintenance of that peace will be given according to the decision of the king's court.

3. Both Dafydd and Gruffudd will hold the portions pertaining to them of the aforesaid lands in chief from the king.

4. He will restore to Roger of Mold, seneschal of Chester, his land of Mold with its appurtenances and to him and other barons of the king the seisin of lands occupied since the war between King John and Llywelyn, saving any right of property contained in an agreement, with this right to be subject to the jurisdiction of the king's court.

5. He will restore to the king all expenses incurred through his campaign.

6. He will make satisfaction for damage and injuries inflicted by him and his men, according to the decision of the aforesaid court, or hand over the malefactors to the king.

7. He will restore to the king all homages which his father John had and which the king ought to have by right, especially those of all Welsh nobles.

8. The king will not abandon any of his adherents and their seisins may remain with the king and his men.

9. The land of Ellesmere with its appurtenances will remain with the king and his heirs for ever and the land of Englefield (Tegeingl) will be kept at his will for himself and his heirs for ever.

10. Henceforth Dafydd will not receive in his land, nor allow to be received, persons outlawed or banished by the king or his barons of the March.

11. He will give security concerning the observance of all the aforesaid articles through hostages, pledges and other means specified by the king.

12. In these and all other matters Dafydd will be at the wish and command of the king and obey the law in all things in his court.

Sealing clause; dating clause.

13. Those who are detained with Gruffudd will be similarly handed over to the king until his court has decided whether and in what manner they ought to be released.

14. In order to uphold all the aforesaid terms Dafydd has sworn on the holy cross that he has carried around with him. Hugh, bishop of St Asaph, at Dafydd's request, has promised on his order to do all the aforesaid things and will ensure that they are observed as far as he is able. Ednyfed Fychan has sworn likewise on the aforesaid cross on Dafydd's orders.

15. Dafydd has further granted that if he or his heirs attempt to contravene the king's peace or the aforesaid articles, their entire inheritance will be forfeit to the king and his heirs.

16. With respect to all these matters Dafydd has placed himself and his heirs under the jurisdiction of the archbishop of Canterbury and the bishops of London, Hereford and Coventry, so that all or any of them may excommunicate him and place an interdict on his land if he should attempt to contravene the aforesaid peace. He has arranged that the bishops of Bangor and St Asaph have given charters to the king in which they agree to carry out all sentences of excommunication or interdict by the aforesaid archbishop and bishops at their command.

Gwerneigron, 29 August 1241.

Source: *The Acts of Welsh Rulers 1120–1283.* Edited by Huw Pryce

The Tower of London
William the Conqueror (King William the First of England, reigned 1066–87) constructed upon the site of former strongholds an imposing Norman castle, initially of timber and later of stone and the large keep we know today as the White Tower still dominates its surroundings. The royal citadel came to be viewed as nothing more than a crucible of terror, a place where out-of-favour members of the British nobility were cast in order to endure a wretched regime of incarceration. Throughout the longitude of the centuries, many members of the Welsh nobility witnessed first-hand the unpleasantries of the dreaded Tower. It was here on the 1st of March, 1244, that Gruffydd ap Llywelyn fell to his death during the procedure of a disastrous attempt to escape from his lofty prison apartment within the Tower. The actual window in which Gruffydd exited before descending to his death can still be viewed today; the window faces the Traitor's Gate and is situated upon the south-west of the tower at the western end of the Chapel.

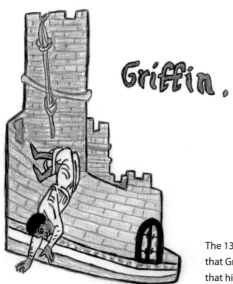

Griffin.

The 13th century chronicler Matthew Paris stated that Gruffydd landed on his head with such force that his neck was crushed between his shoulders.

Tafolwern Castle, near Machynlleth, Powys

The castle was built by Owain Cyfeiliog (c.1130–97), a prince of southern Powys whose fortress formed the chief seat of the commote of Cyfeiliog. Owain's son, Gwenwynwyn, was a great rival to Llywelyn ap Iorwerth and this dangerous feud between the rival princes continued into the next generation as Gwenwynwyn's son, Gruffydd, became an early opponent of Dafydd ap Llywelyn. After the death of his brother, Gruffydd, on the 1st of March 1244, Dafydd summoned the aid of the Welsh princes in anticipation of his expected tussle with King Henry. However, Gruffydd ap Gwenwynwyn of southern Powys defiantly refused to honour this request and during the summer of 1244, Dafydd's army besieged and then successfully captured Gruffydd's manor and castle.

13th century Welsh soldiers (as depicted upon 13th century manuscripts)

Welsh archer (below left)   Welsh spearman (below right)

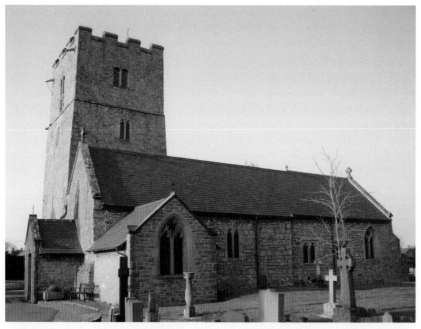

St Michael's Church, Caerwys, Clwyd

As a consequence of an ongoing political dispute between Dafydd and Henry the Third, the English sovereign was summoned to appear before a special hearing at the north-east Wales church in order to respond to listed Welsh grievances. However, on the 20th of January 1245 – the date of the scheduled hearing – King Henry failed to show.

Bailey Hill, Mold, Flintshire

The surviving motte at the former site of Mold Castle is known locally as Bailey Hill. Mold Castle was built during the first part of the 12th century by Anglo-Norman lord, Robert Montallt (de Mohaut). It was subsequently held by his descendants until the early years of the 14th century. However, the castle fell into the determined hands of Welsh forces upon numerous occasions during this period: Prince Owain Gwynedd (winter 1146), Prince Llywelyn ap Iorwerth (January 1199) and Prince Dafydd ap Llywelyn (28 March 1245) being three prime examples. In the successful assault upon Mold Castle (28 March 1245) it is thought that Dafydd's forces may have based their success around the use of catapults in order to batter into submission the fortress held by Roger the Second of Mold.

Dyserth Castle, Denbighshire

Following on from the brief war of 1241 between Wales and England, the victorious Henry the Third reinforced his grip upon a defeated northern Wales by constructing a castle in the hills overlooking Dyserth (or Dissard in its original form). Situated at the northern tip of the Clwydian Range, the castle at Dyserth was built upon a grand scale, many believing that it had considerable similarities with the later castle constructed at Conwy by Henry's son, Edward. Evidently, the castle at Dyserth fell to Dafydd during the Welsh leader's resounding successes in north-east Wales during the spring of 1245. Now almost nothing remains of Dyserth Castle, other than banks and ditch defences belonging to the outer ward. The vast majority of the former site has been quarried away but there still remains a small quantity of scattered stonework.

Deganwy Castle, Gwynedd

Built upon the elevated position of an accommodating duo of imposing rocks overlooking the Conwy estuary, the castle of Deganwy was originally the site of the royal court of 6th century Welsh ruler, Maelgwn Gwynedd. Llywelyn the Great captured from English control a later built fortress upon the site, and whilst in Welsh hands the castle was used to detain Llywelyn's son, Gruffydd, for a period of six years until his release in 1234. During Dafydd ap Llywelyn's later wars against Henry the Third the Welsh prince chose to destroy the castle before it could be taken by English royal forces. However, Henry reoccupied the strategic site during the year 1245 and amidst an exceptionally harsh winter, he began its reconstruction.

Conwy Estuary

A picture taken from the east side of the Conwy estuary at Deganwy looking directly across towards Conwy. A campaigning English soldier writing home during the conflict described the distance between the opposing shores as "a crossbow shot wide".

Church of St Mary and All Saints, Conwy (right)

The present day Conwy parish church, founded in honour of the blessed Virgin Mary and All Saints, was originally the Cistercian Abbey of Aberconwy whose construction was carried out during the reign of Prince Rhodri ab Owain (d. 1195). As well as forming an important depository for Welsh national records ,it became an elected burial place for male members of Gwynedd royalty. Llywelyn the Great was lavishly interred here, as were both of his sons, Gruffydd and Dafydd. It has been estimated that within a quarter of a century of its foundation in 1186, the monastery of Aberconwy had accumulated an estate of nearly 40,000 acres. During 1245, an English army stationed at nearby Deganwy, clearly angered by the plundering of an English supply ship which had ran aground in the Conwy estuary by Welsh soldiers, ransacked the sacred abbey, stealing holy chalices and other valuables before torching the buildings belonging to it. Inside the present day church, there remains no obvious clues to the original location of the former royal mausoleums, all long since removed and destroyed, but the building's east and west end buttresses and parts of the walls, notably on the north side, survive from the structure of the original 12th century abbey church.

English soldiers fighting on campaign in Wales

(Author's personal photograph of an exhibition panel depicting a mediaeval battle; panel located at Castle Mill wood, Chirk, near Wrexham.)

Tomen-y-Rhodwydd Castle, Llandegla, Denbighshire

Built by Dafydd's great-grandfather, Prince Owain Gwynedd, in 1149, the motte and bailey fortification was constructed during the period of Owain Gwynedd's power struggle with Powys and as a marked statement of intent it was erected on the eastern rim of Owain's newly acquired lands near to the reduced Powysian border. However, Iorwerth Goch, a noble of Powys and a brother of Madog ap Maredudd, Prince of Powys, reacted to the boldness of Gwynedd by burning the castle to the ground during the year 1157. As is so often the case, history came to repeat itself when Dafydd ap Llywelyn also found himself embroiled in a conflict with Powys. During this occasion, the feud with Gruffudd ap Gwenwynwyn of southern Powys led to Dafydd's capture of the important Powysian manor of Tafolwern during the summer of 1244.

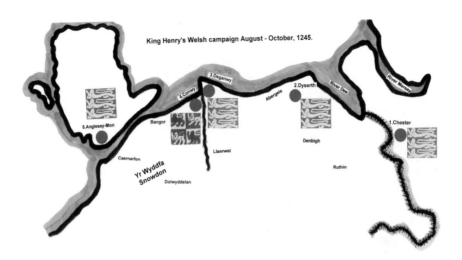

King Henry's Welsh campaign August - October, 1245.

King Henry's Welsh Campaign August–October 1245

1. Chester: 13th August 1245. King Henry arrives in Chester to join up with the main body of his forces. Henry's serving justice of Chester, John Lestrange, initiates the English charge onto Welsh soil, leading the vanguard of the king's army onto the compliant Flintshire plains.

2. Dyserth: Unimpeded, the advancing force of invasion quickly secures the castle of Dyserth as Henry patiently awaits at Chester for news.

3. Deganwy: 26th August 1245. Establishing a 50 mile long supply line from his garrison base at Chester, Henry – now at the helm of all field operations – halts his forces upon the east bank of the Conwy estuary at Deganwy. Here, he begins the reconstruction of the abandoned Welsh castle upon the summit of Deganwy hill, left ruinous due to the policy of deliberate demolition on the part of Dafydd's defending army.

4. Conwy: Dafydd has adequately prepared himself for a lengthy campaign and in anticipation of the English onslaught, his Welsh forces of defence are firmly dug in upon the opposing bank of the estuary at Conwy.

5. Anglesey/Môn: Henry's aim is to crush all modes of resistance employed by Dafydd and the king initiates a two-pronged assault against Gwynedd. His mainland troops stationed at Deganwy are joined in the theatre of war by 3,000 allied troops despatched from Ireland. The marine force is instructed to invade the Isle of Anglesey, which it does successfully.

* As war unfolds, a devastating tussle of attrition materialises as the Welsh winter descends harsh and early. Atrocities are willingly committed by both sides. English forces plunder the revered abbey of Aberconwy, removing precious valuables and other sacred relics, whilst the Welsh respond with rage – hanging and dismembering all captured English prisoners-of-war. Frustrated by the lack of military success and progress in the field impeded further by the ravages of perhaps the cruellest of Welsh winters, Henry decides to withdraw from Deganwy on 26th October 1245, leaving behind his flagging garrison to combat the incessant forces of bitter frosts and furious vengeance.

Llys Euryn, Llandrillo-yn-Rhos (Rhos-on-Sea), near Colwyn Bay
Ednyfed Fychan was the seneschal or chief steward of Dafydd ap Llywelyn's royal council and previously he had fulfilled that very same role for the father, Llywelyn the Great. Ednyfed was a loyal and highly-respected servant to Gwynedd's royal house and in 1230, he acquired the lands of Rhos Fynach by way of a royal charter. Upon those lands at a place called Bryn Euryn, Ednyfed built a fortified Hall called Llys Euryn – the Court of the Golden Hill. Although the mediaeval ruins on top of Bryn Euryn hill consist chiefly of limestone blocks that are dated to a later period than Ednyfed's lifetime, it is believed that the grindstones affixed to the wall of the West Hall are materials that once belonged to Ednyfed's original 13th century structure.

The parish church of Llandrillo-yn-Rhos, Colwyn Bay

The oldest part of the existing church is the north aisle, which is believed to have been the private chapel of Ednyfed Fychan (d. 1246), seneschal to the princes of Gwynedd during the first period of the 13th century. Ednyfed's manor house was located within the same vicinity upon the summit of Bryn Euryn hill several hundred yards to the south. Many believe that the inscribed sepulchral slab currently located upon the porch wall of the historic church – bearing the name of Ednyfed – is the actual tomb stone of Ednyfed Fychan.

The coat-of-arms of Ednyfed Fychan (d. 1246) – seneschal or chief steward to Prince Dafydd ap Llywelyn. A chevron between three decapitated heads of Englishmen/Saxons. Ednyfed, as seneschal of Gwynedd was, simultaneously, the prince's chief financial agent, leading judge and chief executive officer.

Penrhyn Castle, Bangor, Gwynedd

During his lengthy tenure as the serving seneschal or chief minister of the royal council of Gwynedd, Ednyfed Fychan was granted generous estates of land throughout northern Wales, including a tract of land that lay to the east of Bangor called Penrhyn – meaning "headland". In all probability, Ednyfed Fychan constructed the first established residence upon the site that the existing Penrhyn Castle now occupies. Ednyfed Fychan died during the year 1246, and at least two, possibly three, of his sons followed their highly respected father as stewards of the princes of Gwynedd.

During the war of 1244–46, Prince Dafydd's nephew, Llywelyn ap Gruffydd evolved to fulfil the important role of a trusted military adjutant to his uncle's service. Of the four sons of his half-brother Gruffydd, Llywelyn was regarded as Dafydd's personal favourite and became ever-present during the period of the demanding conflict. (Image of Prince Llywelyn reproduced by author from Prince Llywelyn Inn, Cilmeri.)

Shotwick Castle, near Chester, Cheshire

The motte and bailey castle at Shotwick, later to be blessed by the addition of six stone towers, was strategically established upon a steep escarpment above the east bank of the river Dee. Guarding an ancient ford that led into Wales, whereupon English armies of invasion could readily transgress into Wales, the Norman-established border castle played an integral part of the Anglo-Welsh wars of the mediaeval age. After the death of his uncle, Prince Dafydd of Gwynedd, on the 25th of February 1246, Owain Goch – an elder brother to Llywelyn ap Gruffydd – successfully fled from his captors at Shotwick Castle in order to ride the short distance into Wales to pursue his rightful claim to an equal share of the princedom of Gwynedd.

Shotwick Castle, near Chester, Cheshire

Blenheim Palace, Woodstock, Oxfordshire

Twelve months after the death of Prince Dafydd, Welsh resistance – spearheaded by Dafydd's two nephews, Llywelyn and Owain – finally crumpled when English royal forces led by Nicholas de Molis reached Deganwy unopposed during the spring of 1247. On the 5th of March 1247, a five-week truce was arranged with the king's justiciar of Chester, John de Grey, and during this period of military inactivity, a safe conduct was granted to the two Welsh princes for their visit to confer with the king at Oxford (Thursday, 18th of April 1247). Consequently, the surrender and final submission was confirmed by the signing of the Treaty of Woodstock on the 30th of April 1247. The historic treaty between Henry the Third and Princes Llywelyn and Owain was signed, sealed and delivered inside the palace of Woodstock, an English royal residence near Oxford. Woodstock Palace was later destroyed during the English Civil War, and the existing Blenheim Palace was built upon the site.

King Henry the Third's gilt-bronze tomb-effigy in Westminster Abbey. Dafydd's formidable foe, Henry the Third survived a further twenty-six years after the death of his opponent, eventually meeting his own end on 16th November 1272. The English sovereign was buried inside Westminster Abbey, a building which he lavishly rebuilt during a reign that lasted an incredible fifty-six years.

Edward, the eldest child of Henry the Third and Eleanor of Provence, was Dafydd's first cousin and being born on 17th June 1239, he was only six years old at the time of the Welsh prince's death. Edward later succeeded his father, Henry the Third, as king and quickly forged a reputation of being a devout and bitter opponent of Dafydd's nephew and successor, Prince Llywelyn ap Gruffydd. (Author's personal photograph of a painted image near to the high altar in Westminster Abbey believed to be King Edward the First.)

OES AUR TYWYSOGION GWYNEDD
"Pura Wallia"
1137 - 1283

Owain ap Gruffudd
Llywelyn ap Iorwerth
Dafydd ap Llywelyn
Llywelyn ap Gruffudd
Dafydd ap Gruffudd
a'i feibion
y tywysogion ifanc
Llywelyn ac Owain

Church of St Peter ad Vincula, Pennal, near Machynlleth

It was at Pennal, during Lent 1406 that Prince Owain Glyndŵr (Prince of Wales, 1400–15) formulated the important national document known to historians as the Pennal Policy. Some two centuries beforehand, Prince Llywelyn the Great presided over his own council of chiefs at nearby Aberdyfi, during the year 1216. In acknowledgement of these important links between the Welsh princes and this area of southern Gwynedd, the church of St Peter ad Vincula in the village of Pennal, near Machynlleth has established a commemorative garden in honour of listed members of Welsh royalty. The name of Dafydd ap Llywelyn, Prince of Wales, forms part of the tasteful tribute.

78

Prince Dafydd Plaque of Commemoration, Bagillt, Flintshire

To celebrate the historic birth of the former Prince of Wales within the mediaeval manor of Coleshill, now a part of the modern-day Flintshire village of Bagillt, a commemorative plaque was unveiled upon the outside wall of the Upper Shippe public house on the 25th of July 2010, to honour Prince Dafydd who was born at the nearby former Welsh royal residence of Castell Hen Blas sometime during or around the year 1215. The ceremony was attended by 250 people and the plaque was unveiled by Mr Dafydd Wigley, honorary President of Plaid Cymru.

ER COF AM 'TARIAN CYMRU'   IN MEMORY OF 'THE SHIELD OF WALES'

DAFYDD II AP LLYWELYN

GANWYD YNG NGHASTELL HEN BLAS   BORN IN HEN BLAS CASTLE

TYWYSOG CYMRU 1240-46   PRINCE OF WALES 1240-46

A ANFONODD LYSGENHADON   WHO SENT AMBASSADORS TO THE
AT FRENIN FFRAINC A'R PAB;   KING OF FRANCE AND THE POPE,
GORCHFYGODD HARRI III,   AND DEFEATED HENRY III,
BRENIN LLOEGR, YN 1245   KING OF ENGLAND, IN 1245

NODDWR ABATY DINAS BASING;   PATRON OF BASINGWERK ABBEY;
AROLYGWR CYFRAITH HYWEL   REVISER OF THE LAWS OF HYWEL
DDA; GWLEIDYDD, RHYFELWR   DDA; STATESMAN, WARRIOR
A GWLADGARWR   AND PATRIOT

- III -

By confidently marshalling a powerful military alliance that contained an extraordinary wealth of talent drawn from each corner of Wales, Dafydd had duly afforded himself the grandest opportunity to date of attempting to banish forever the painful memory of his humiliating surrender at Gwern Eigron in 1241. The dream team of princes and magnates that flocked to his purposely raised standard of revolt more than matched anything that Wales had ever seen before. From even the remotest territories of the distant south, the leading nobles had all pledged their support. The considerable support from Glamorgan included Rhys ap Gruffydd of Senghennydd, Hywel ap Maredudd of Meisgyn and also the sons of Morgan Gam in Afan. Further additions to the chemistry of the potent mix included Maredudd ap Owain of Ceredigion, Maredudd ap Rhys of Dryslwyn in Carmarthenshire, Rhys Fychan of Dinefwr and Maelgwn Fychan of northern Ceredigion, who had all thrown their collective weight behind Dafydd. In central Wales, native Welsh lords Maredudd ap Maelgwn and Hywel ap Cadwallon also embraced the challenge and willingly sided with the expanding cause of Welsh unity. Between them, the allied forces of Wales scooped victory after victory in their net of conquest. During February 1245, an English force that had been actively scouring the area of the south under the leadership of Herbert Fitz Matthew, suddenly found itself outflanked by a unit of Welsh soldiery during the manoeuvre of what proved to be a devastating ambush. During the ensuing sanguinary encounter, Fitz Matthew was himself slain, alongside a greater part of his company as they attempted to negotiate a hill pass near Margam in the district of Nedd (Neath) upon the southern coast of Wales. On the 28th of March 1245, the strategically important garrison town of Mold (Yr Wyddgrug), which is situated only ten miles in distance from the city of Chester and the

English border, was sensationally taken, together with its hilltop castle, by Dafydd and his determined force. During the assault upon Lord Roger the Second of Mold's castle, it is believed that Dafydd built the foundation of his success upon the effective use of catapults in order to reduce the hill top garrison to a state of submission. Catapults during warfare were first used by the ancient Greeks and Romans, and these attacking and much feared engines of war had to be placed at a distance of at least 300 yards from the walls of a target in order to prove reliable and to deliver success. Given Dafydd's emerging capacity for statesmanship and the magnetic force of his charisma, it was little wonder that each and every member of his father's highly respected former council continued to remain loyal to the son's service throughout the entirety of his short, but eventful reign. Furthermore, Dafydd, at this stage, had even been accredited with securing the personal services of Llywelyn ap Gruffydd, the second born son of his deceased brother, Gruffydd, who, being Dafydd's royal nephew and personal favourite continued to perform an active and enthusiastic duty as one of his uncle's trusted and ever-present war captains during the course of the escalating conflict. During this period of agitation, Dafydd successfully regained most of the territories in north-east Wales that he had so meekly surrendered during the war of 1241. In all probability, the Denbighshire castle of Dyserth, near Rhuddlan, was also seized by Dafydd's forces during the Welsh renaissance. However, the recent Welsh activity was not without its reverses, as up to 300 Welshmen were reported slaughtered during a bloody border engagement near Montgomery in Powys, delivering a temporary setback to the overwhelming success of the Welsh revival.

The fine steeds were languid with the toils of the day,
When the hosts wallowed in gore and were thrown into confusion.
The bow was fully bent towards its victim;
The shaft aimed at the breast in the region of Northop.
The army at Offa's Dyke panted for glory;

The troops of North Wales and the men of London

Were as the alternate motion of the waves on the seashore;

When the sea-mew (seagull) screams,

Our happiness was great in the defeat of the Normans.

Verse written by Welsh bard Einion ap Gwgon, *c*.1244

Dafydd suffered an even greater and far more defining setback when he received the startling news that the Pope had performed the manoeuvre of an astonishing U-turn regarding the future cause of Wales. In a disgraceful turn of events, Pope Innocent the Fourth decidedly dismissed the Welsh grievances and alternatively he chose in favour of King Henry's England. The abandoned Dafydd was left stunned by the snub. In a Papal correspondence addressed to the English bishops of Ely and Carlisle, dated at Lyons on the 8th of April 1245, the stinging rebuke declared that the royal ancestors of Dafydd ap Llywelyn had always been regarded as the recognised duty-bound vassals of the King of England. The alluring promise of a plentiful supply of English gold had obviously proved too tempting of an offer to resist. With Papal support successfully secured, Henry diverted his immediate energies into overcoming the pressing Welsh challenge.

Any purposeful study of modern day history writings relating to the figure of King Henry the Third of England (ruled 1216–72) will inevitably lead the student towards a catalogue of uncomplimentary accounts concerning Henry's character and reign. Penned by the hand of respected English historians, the damning indictments freely flow. Professor David Loades writing in *Kings and Queens* describes Henry as "a poor king"; Henry fares no better in the written work *A Pageant of History* by W M Collins with "he was rather a weak king, who did some incredibly foolish things". Josephine Ross writing in *Monarchs of Britain* does not hold back either, declaring him "A king who had major failings: he was weak, unreliable, extravagant and dangerously insensitive to the feelings of his subjects". Nevertheless, the reigning King of England was a devout enemy of Gwynedd and encouraged by his own self-confidence – which in Henry was never lacking – he had decided in favour of initiating a summer campaign against the rebellious Dafydd, to which the sovereign himself would lead an army onto the field of battle. On the 13th of August 1245, Henry marched into Wales. In pursuit of the final subjugation of Gwynedd, the English monarch had summoned the entire muster of his impressive knighthood service. The campaign of invasion began at the gates of the former Roman citadel of Chester, where Henry's impressive modern-day legion marched westwards in pursuit of a speedy victory. The Clwydian terrain had not altered since Henry's last triumphant thrust into Wales some four years previous, but the demeanour of his enemy certainly had. Dafydd had learned some vital lessons from the errors that he had previously committed during the first conflict of 1241, in which he had been completely out-witted within the area of the war zone. Never again would Dafydd allow himself to commit the cardinal sin of leaving the gateway to Snowdonia unprotected and thereby isolating himself and his army from this natural structure of defence. This time, he would use the imposing and rugged mountainous frontier as his very first line of defence.

The experienced Henry began his war campaign impressively, quickly securing the English-built castle of Dyserth, near Rhuddlan, before establishing a fifty mile long supply line, the winding sinews of which stretched from the gates of Chester to the banks of the Conwy river. King Henry crossed the Clwydian frontier spreading with him a destructive cocktail of fire and ruin, only ceasing the hostilities once he had reached the stronghold of Deganwy upon the eastern bank of the Conwy estuary. However, the retreating Dafydd had already reduced the castle of Deganwy that had been freshly taken by Henry to a heap of rubble and ruin. Now camped upon the eastern side of the Conwy estuary, the English force busied themselves with the urgent reconstruction of a new fortress upon the rugged twin peaks of Deganwy hill. Anxious to avoid an open and full-scale confrontation against a vastly superior number, Dafydd had deployed his forces of defence upon the opposite bank of the Conwy estuary. With the front line established, the enveloping war of attrition turned ugly. Sun-kissed arable acres were transformed overnight into fire scorched meadows as both sides jostled desperately for a source of supremacy. Nightly, the Welsh attacked beneath the cover of diamond encrusted skies, they slaughtered and then skillfully withdrew into the shadows; whilst the English soldiery saw fit to ransack the nearby abbey of Aberconwy, where they pilfered a quantity of the prized treasures that were held inside its precincts. In an attempt to deprive Dafydd of his vital provisions – including the crop supply that helped nourish his army – a sea-borne force was dispatched from Ireland and upon Henry's orders the 3,000-strong marine force were tasked to raid the island of Anglesey; and during this period of frenzied activity not one step backwards did either side negotiate. Describing the conditions of camp, a contemporary English cleric-chronicler, Matthew Paris (d. 1259), uses a direct quotation from a letter belonging to an English soldier serving on the front line, "There is a small arm of the sea, which ebbs and flows under the castle, and forming a sort of harbour into which, during our stay here, ships have often come from Ireland and Chester, bringing provisions. This arm of the sea lies between us and Snowdon, where the Welsh quarter themselves, and is, at high tide, about a crossbow (shot) wide." The same serving soldier further records how during the experience of a violent attack upon themselves by Welsh soldiers enraged by the plundering of the revered abbey of Aberconwy, a great number of his fellow men were forced to flee the melee by casting themselves directly to the judgement of the foaming waves.

During the year 1245, the fierce grip of winter descended early upon the land of Wales and it would prove to be the severest for many a decade. A coruscated sheet of brilliant white frost cast its spell upon the land, transforming the harmless green terrain of mid autumn into a shocking Arctic wilderness as a devilish alliance of wild blustery blizzards and bitterly cold frosts proceeded to torment the resident soldiery huddled upon both sides of the Conwy river. The English rank and file were accommodated within the community of their makeshift tented camps and, upon the exposed eastern bank, they were haplessly cursed by the persistent chill factor, which bit deep and gnawed ever so cruel into the exposed flesh of the shivering combatants. In fact, the only visible thing that appeared to thaw above the frozen ground was man's ever vulnerable spirit. Ravaged by exposure – food, clothing and adequate shelter regarded as none other than the most envied of commodities – the morale of the English invader began to plummet as drastically as the freezing temperatures.

Despite the extreme weather conditions, raids, ambushes, bloodshed and wanton slaughter continued, the war zone being no different to any other as the gruesome, twisted corpses of both armies slain lay littered amidst the killing fields of Deganwy and Conwy. A duty-bound cargo ship sailing into the perilous waters of Conwy Bay unexpectedly ran aground beneath the landmark site of the newly constructed castle of Deganwy, resulting in both armies indulging in a desperate struggle for the sought after treasures of its hold. Shocking scenes ensued as the factions fought like rabid dogs, the victors of the sickening hand-to-hand clashes scurrying away with plentiful supplies of stolen food and wine. By choosing to make a defiant stand upon the banks of the river Conwy, the resilient Dafydd had successfully halted the progress of Henry's advancement. Frustrated by the fruitlessness of an ongoing stalemate, in which both forces had become haplessly embroiled in a tussle of attrition, Henry physically removed himself from the chaos of the war zone and vowed to resume his campaign afresh during the following season of spring. Leaving behind a small garrison at Deganwy castle, the bedraggled body of men that Henry led back to the sanctuary of the English border during the final days of October 1245, was a half-starved mockery of the mighty host which had confidently marched out of the gates of Chester only two months before. Even the king's amphibious force that had been launched from Ireland with instructions to ravage Anglesey had suffered heavy losses, before it too was forced to withdraw from the theatre of war by that same month's ending.

Henry brushed aside the disappointment of his failed campaign of invasion and attempted to bring the defiant Dafydd and his Welsh allies to their knees by the employment of an alternative strategy. He ordered a full trade embargo against the region of northern Wales, the cradle of Welsh resistance. The essential provisions of salt, corn, steel, iron and woven cloth, which were usually imported from England, were to be denied the region in a determined drive to bring a stubborn opponent closer to submission. During the course of the all too brief war of August 1241, Dafydd feebly conceded without even the dignity of a defined fight. However, during the latest hostilities, he had so far refused to buckle and despite the northern province being deprived of some of its crucial nutrients his confident leadership continued to resist a superior power. As time wore on, the debilitating effects of the embargo gave rise to a harvest of fear and uncertainty and inevitably, the Welsh revival would soon terminate, but the dawn of defeat arrived via the most unlikely of circumstances, and dramatically so.

The ruling sovereign of Wales lay stricken upon what would soon prove to be the scene of his death bed. Ravaged by the debilitating effects of a high fever, the prostrate leader of Wales struggled intensely amidst the bondage of his bed sheets. The endless, black void of oblivion loomed ever closer as his weakened body desperately fought for the breath of sustained life. Inside the prince's private chambers at Llys Garth Celyn, Abergwyngregyn, the hot candle wax dripped from flickering lanterns as the tapestry clad walls of his inner sanctum excitedly came to life with a demonic display of dark, dancing shadows. Throughout the royal complex, the grim stench of death courted company with the cool night air of early spring as Wales' head of state – now deep in delirium – duly entered the final phase of a crippling affliction; a condition later described by the prince's inner circle as "the sweating sickness". According to contemporary accounts, the symptoms of his illness had already caused him to lose a proportion of his scalp hair; and its latter affects had also emaciated some of his fingers and toes. The pure theatre produced by Dafydd's swirling descent towards the gaping jaws of death had understandably attracted a conglomerate of the elder statesmen of Gwynedd. In line with royal protocol, the Prince of Wales' personal retainers were all present at the gloom induced vigil, including trusted members of the household's elitist armed corps of bodyguard known as the *teulu*, his serving seneschal from nearby Penrhyn, the clergy from Bangor, personal attendants and duty-bound scriveners. In a confederation of chilled silence, they had dutifully gathered at their sovereign's royal residence in order to await the formality of the cessation of a royal life. Of course, his loyal wife and princess, Lady Isabella de Braose, was also on hand to witness the final voyage of her husband's premature surrender.

History duly records that upon the twenty-fifth day of February, during the year 1246, Prince Dafydd the Second of Wales breathed his last and thereupon ended another trauma ridden chapter of Welsh history. With a grieving Wales still officially at war with England – the horrors of which had tragically besmeared the northern lands of the Cymry with a virus of death, famine and destruction – the death of Dafydd greatly strengthened Henry's position against an already weakened Wales. In various contemporary circles, there existed disturbing rumours that Dafydd had somehow been poisoned by the treacherous will of his enemies who resided in England. Frustrated by their failure to overcome the rugged Dafydd militarily, the theory survives in the minds of many that a vine of conspiracy could in fact have taken root from inside the very precincts of King Henry's royal court. Furthermore, the convenient timing of Dafydd's death could be viewed in some quarters with a credible degree of suspicion as being the typical hallmark of a deliberate and carefully engineered plot.

Various other theories abound in relation to the possible cause of Dafydd's premature death. Concurrent bouts of alopecia and onycholysis, and even leprosy were cast as considered culprits that could either have contributed to or directly led to the young prince's startling decline and subsequent death. The lingering seeds of suspicion surrounding Dafydd's death subsequently germinated to create an impenetrable veil that still exists in the modern day. The death of such a young royal sovereign was made even more tragic by the fact that Dafydd departed the platform of life without even the benefit of leaving behind a natural born successor and immediate heir.

Dafydd fittingly received a dignified state funeral and he was laid to rest inside a magnificent crafted tomb that was placed alongside the sarcophagus that contained the remains of his illustrious father, Llywelyn the Great, within the abbey church of Aberconwy. Months later, Dafydd's childless, widowed wife, Lady Isabella de Braose, returned to her ancestral homelands before succumbing herself to a premature death sometime during or around the year 1248. To her eternal credit, Dafydd's royal consort had served the royal court of Gwynedd with both dignity and distinction for a period of sixteen years. A short time after Dafydd's death, his nephew, Owen Goch, escaped from his captors at Shotwick Castle upon the banks of the river Dee near Chester, where he had been closely supervised since the beginning of Henry's second war with Dafydd. Upon fleeing into Wales, the eldest born son of Gruffydd ap Llywelyn urgently sought an audience with his younger brother, Llywelyn who, during this same period, was actively campaigning for the support of the native princes in order to continue the struggle against Henry. However, without the benefit of Dafydd's guile and leadership, the Welsh war effort collapsed as the English war machine proceeded to trample across Wales unopposed. One by one, Dafydd's allies were toppled. Henry had sent Nicholas de Myles (or Molis), his justice of Carmarthen in south-west Wales to forcibly regain the lands of Maelgwn Fychan in northern Ceredigion. Unimpeded on the western coast of Wales, he then led his army northwards upon a victorious march towards the river Dyfi and beyond, not halting his force until they had amalgamated with the garrison at Deganwy. During this same period, the Earl of Clare dispossessed Hywel ap Maredudd of his territory in Glamorgan, causing the native southern leader to flee northwards to the mountainous sanctuary of Gwynedd and the protection of its royal court. Prince Dafydd's nephews, Llywelyn and Owen decided that any future resistance would be futile and on the 5th of March 1247, their elected envoys met John de Grey, the king's justice of Chester for the purpose of a truce. Some eight weeks later, at the palace of Woodstock, an English royal residence situated five miles north-west of Oxford, the capitulation was confirmed by the signing of the Treaty of Woodstock on the 30th of April 1247.

In various Welsh history circles, the reign of Dafydd ap Llywelyn is often overlooked by those individuals who choose instead to favour the more romantic and seemingly more colourful episodes of Welsh mediaeval history, namely the golden eras associated with such heavyweights as Owain Gwynedd, the two Llywelyns and Owain Glyndŵr. Perhaps this ignorance is due to the fact that Dafydd's tenure as ruling prince only lasted for a brief period of six years and this partly explains why the story of his career and lifetime is somewhat shrouded in mystery. And yet, during the period of those same six years, the charismatic figure that Dafydd ap Llywelyn undoubtedly was, successfully gained the respect of some of the most important and influential figures of that age, including the elected papal leader of the Catholic Church, the King of France, Louis IX; the senior clergymen of Wales, the majority of the lesser Welsh princes, and more importantly, he managed to successfully retain the loyal support of each and every member of his father's former royal council. Furthermore, he successfully held at bay the periodic threat posed by his capricious half-brother, Gruffydd; he became the first Welsh royal leader to confidently invest himself to the supreme title of Prince of Wales; and within the period of his short reign, he contested two wars against superior numbers, even managing during the second of those conflicts to regain vast tracts of land in north-east Wales through the medium of fire and sword. Neither should the fact be ignored that during the latter phase of Dafydd's reign, his inexperienced nephew of teenage years,

Llywelyn ap Gruffydd, benefited greatly from the intimate apprenticeship he received courtesy of the guiding hand of his royal uncle, to which the young Llywelyn – a man who would later himself become the recognised and commendable national leader of Welsh Wales – witnessed first-hand the daily and often rigorous demands that accompanied successful royal governance. Shortly after the death of Dafydd ap Llywelyn, the influential court poet, Dafydd Benfras, composed a sombre and dignified elegy in his honour. Part of the elegy translates as:

> The hand which last year held the breach;
>
> At Aberconwy until put to rest:
>
> Grandson of the King of England, from a host of kings;
>
> Son of the King of Wales, of steadfast lineage;
>
> He was a man who sprang, great joy of the people;
>
> From the true lineage of kings:

Other complimentary lines included: "There was not as good a man under God as was Dafydd" and "There was no Welshman his equal". The poignant tribute should be considered even more remarkable by the fact that only five years before its production, the respected scribe was a renowned opponent of the Welsh prince. Moreover, the magnitude of Dafydd's spectacular and meteoric rise was indelibly confirmed amidst the pages of *Brut y Tywysogion* – The Chronicle of the Princes when a writer of the ancient manuscript emphatically refers to Dafydd as *Tarian Cymru* meaning the Shield of Wales. In the world of patriotism, politics and power, there is no greater epitaph that could ever be inscribed upon the surface of one's tomb.

Within a year of the signing of the Treaty of Woodstock, the body of Gruffydd ap Llywelyn was exhumed from its London burial plot to be transferred to the abbey of Aberconwy and there dutifully laid to rest alongside the glittering tombs of the father and half-brother. Dafydd

Benfras composed a praise lavished elegy in a tribute to all three. Translated as follows:

> Three of the finest warriors among warriors,
>
> Three worthy men whom God has taken from among men,
>
> Three astonishing men causing calamity for the fallen enemy by their fierceness,
>
> Three whose deeds none others can match,
>
> Three gentle men, finest of chieftains,
>
> Three signal ones, swift to assert their rights,
>
> Three heroes, a fine defence for gold-torqued warriors,
>
> Three eagles as men and youths,
>
> Three wounds I bear that they now as Cynon of yore,
>
> Three with spears swift like the flow of the river Peryddon,
>
> Three with blades sharp upon helmeted men,
>
> Three defenders of their land against traitors.

Almost eight centuries have passed since the colourful events of Dafydd's lifetime, but clearly his countrymen have not forgotten the era of his reign. In 2009, a medal was awarded in his name to the writer of the best history essay written by a Welsh language learner at the North East Wales Learners' Eisteddfod. The prize of 'Medal Dafydd ap Llywelyn' is now an annual occurrence at this event. During the same year (2009), Dafydd was immortalised in the night sky by the naming of minor planet 18349 in his honour upon the sanction of an official body of astronomers. In 2010, a plaque of commemoration was unveiled near to the scene of his birthplace in the village of Bagillt in Flintshire, and one year laer came the successful publication of this work.

Thankfully, the name Dafydd ap Llywelyn shall forever be remembered.

The Author wishes to acknowledge the following sources:

Brut y Tywysogion (Chronicle of the Princes) – Thomas Jones

The Welsh Princes 1063–1283 – Roger Turvey

The Monarchs of Britain – Josephine Ross

Flint Castle & Ewloe Castle Guidebook – Cadw

Kings and Queens – David Loades

Wales, Castles and Historic Places – Cadw

The Lord Rhys, Prince of Deheubarth – Roger Turvey

A History of Wales – John Davies

Land of my Fathers – Gwynfor Evans

Glyndŵr's War – G J Brough

Wales, History of a Nation – David Ross

'Remembering the Shield of Wales' – Dr Craig Owen Jones
(article included within *Cambria* magazine, May/June 2009)

Castles of the Welsh Princes – Paul R Davis

Wales, her origins, struggles and later history institutions and manners – Huw Pryce

Who's Who in Welsh History – Deborah C Fisher

Llywelyn the Great – Roger Turvey

The Welsh Wars of Independence – David Moore

The Môn Trail – Menter Môn

The Taming of the Dragon. Edward the First and the Conquest of Wales – W B Bartlett

Royal Visits and Progresses to Wales – Edward Parry

The History of Wales – J Graham Jones

Bagillt through the ages – Bagillt History Club

An Introduction to the History of Wales, Volume 2 – A H Williams

History of Northop – Thomas Edwards

The Welsh Kings, Warriors, Warlords and Princes – Kari Maund

The Poets of the Princes – J E Caerwyn Williams

'Dafydd Benfras and his Red Book Poems' – N Bosco (article within *Studia Celtica* 1987/88)

Wales; Her origins, Struggles and Later History, Institutions and Manners – Gilbert Stone

The Acts of Welsh Rulers (1120–1283) –Huw Pryce

The History of the River Dee – Mike Griffiths

Also available from Y Lolfa:

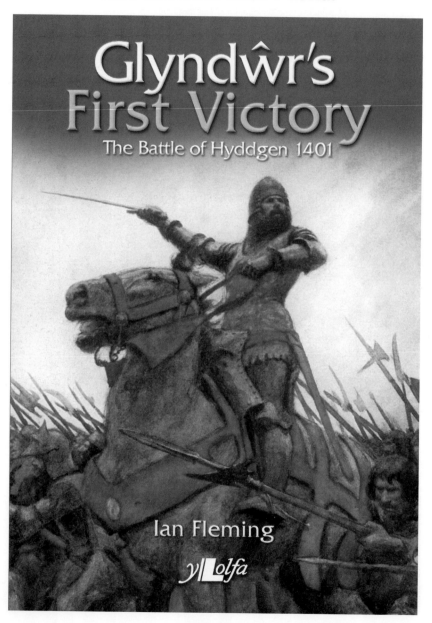

Glyndŵr's
First Victory
The Battle of Hyddgen 1401

Ian Fleming

y Lolfa

£6.95

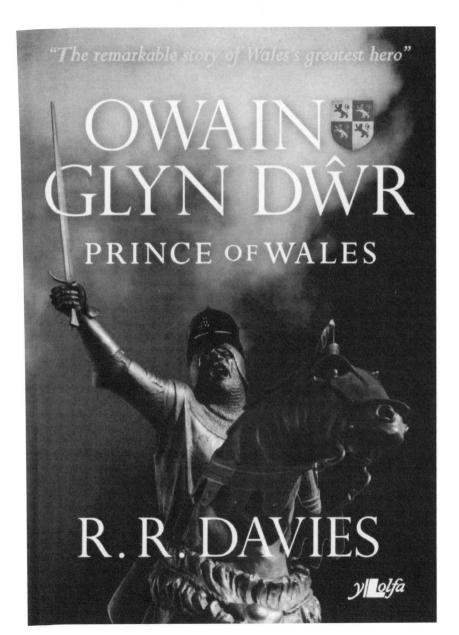

"The remarkable story of Wales's greatest hero"

OWAIN
GLYN DŴR
PRINCE OF WALES

R. R. DAVIES

y Lolfa

£5.95

Dafydd ap Llywelyn is just one of a whole range of publications from Y Lolfa. For a full list of books currently in print, send now for your free copy of our new full-colour catalogue. Or simply surf into our website

www.ylolfa.com

for secure on-line ordering.

Talybont Ceredigion Cymru SY24 5HE
e-mail ylolfa@ylolfa.com
website www.ylolfa.com
phone (01970) 832 304
fax 832 782